INSIDE BROADCASTING

Inside Broadcasting provides a comprehensive introduction to a highly rewarding yet competitive industry. It analyses the day-to-day running of both television and radio organisations and examines the jobs involved and how to get them.

Inside Broadcasting begins with an informative history of broadcasting in the United Kingdom. It traces the invention of radio and television, from the founding of the BBC and ITV networks through to the end of the terrestrial monopoly and the advent of satellite and pay-per-view television.

Julian Newby explains what skills, experience and professional qualifications are required for entry into the broadcasting industry. He provides detailed job descriptions and explains how each job fits into the industry as a whole. Practical careers advice together with a comprehensive list of training and educational bodies, companies and professional publications ensure that *Inside Broadcasting* is an essential introduction to a career in radio and television.

Julian Newby is a writer, broadcaster and consultant on all aspects of the international media. He has worked for independent television in the UK, and produced programmes for LBC Radio, London. He contributes to the careers section of the *Daily Mail* and is co-author of *Inside the Music Business*.

CAREER BUILDERS GUIDES

Inside Journalism
Sara Niblock

Inside the Music Business
Tony Barrow and Julian Newby

Inside Book Publishing
Giles Clark

Inside Broadcasting
Julian Newby

INSIDE
BROADCASTING

Julian Newby

London and New York

First published 1997
by Routledge
11 New Fetter Lane, London EC4P 4EE

Simultaneously published in the USA and Canada
by Routledge
29 West 35th Street, New York, NY 10001

Phototypeset in Times by Intype London Ltd
Printed and bound in Great Britain by T.J. International Ltd, Padstow,
Cornwall

British Library Cataloguing in Publication Data
A catalogue record for this book is available from the British Library

Library of Congress Cataloging in Publication Data
Newby, Julian
Inside Broadcasting/Julian Newby.
p. cm. – (Career Builders Guides)
Simultaneously published in Canada.
Includes bibliographical references and index.
1. Broadcasting – Vocational guidance – Great Britain.   I. Title.
II. Series.
PN1990.55.N46   1997
384.54′023′41 – dc20   96–23975

ISBN 0–415–15771–4 (hbk)
0–415–15112–0 (pbk)

This book is dedicated to Ian Alcoran and
Dan Douglas

CONTENTS

CONTENTS

ACKNOWLEDGEMENTS

The author would like to thank the following people and organisations for their help with the preparation and writing of this book:

Tony Barrow
Clive Bull
Neil Churchman
Mary Collins
Jeremy Coopman
Ian Denyer
Brian Hayes
Debbie Lincoln
Jack Newby

BECTU
The BFI
The ITC
PACT
The Radio Authority
Skillset

1

INTRODUCTION

Few days go by during which you don't come into contact with
the world of broadcasting. Even as you read the first words of
this book for the first time, you will probably have already heard
something on the radio, or seen something on the television. You
might not have turned on that radio or that television yourself;
it might not have been yours at all. The television might have
been one that was on in a shop as you walked past; the radio
might have been playing on a building site, in a shop or someone
else's car. And whatever you heard or saw might well not have
registered with you – but it was there, and you did not escape it.

That is the power of broadcasting. It creates events which affect
us all, whether or not it is our intention to experience them. To
take an obvious example, the interview with the Princess of Wales
which was broadcast as part of the BBC's *Panorama* series in
November 1995 had become a worldwide event some weeks
before it was broadcast. Whether or not it was your intention to
watch it, it was hard to escape press speculation as the broadcast
date approached. And even those who weren't among the 22
million or so British people who watched the interview as it was
broadcast would have had problems escaping the repeated post
mortem it went through in the weeks which followed. I was not
in the UK when the interview went out on air, and thought I had
escaped the whole event when, while I was on an aeroplane
heading for Hong Kong two weeks after the broadcast, it turned
up on the in-flight video programme.

The Princess of Wales interview is, of course, an extreme case,
but nonetheless serves to illustrate the extent to which radio and
television broadcasts have become almost as important to our
lives as the water that comes out of the tap.

This is the principal reason why jobs in broadcasting are considered so appealing – and are therefore quite hard to come by. With a job in broadcasting you could become famous – or at least work with the famous. With a job in broadcasting your work could be heard or seen by millions. As a television scriptwriter or broadcast journalist your words would reach many more people than those of an author or newspaper reporter. As a hard-nosed radio or television interviewer you could bring down the government; as a documentary film maker you could change the world. Get a job on a late-night television chat show and you too could become one of the beautiful people who get photographed with the rich and famous; get a job on a daytime chat show and you could become a household name.

All these thoughts go through the minds of all those who – at whatever stage in their lives – consider working in broadcasting. Except for the privileged few, however, they are idle thoughts. Because for every high-profile talk show host there are a thousand people who want that job; for every award-winning documentary film director there are a thousand others whose job it is to direct the less significant but nonetheless essential pieces of film which fill the remaining 23 hours of the day's schedule; for every earth-shattering piece of investigative journalism there are a thousand weather reports, programme links and introductions to be written; and for every person who appears on camera or behind a microphone there are tens and even hundreds of people working behind the scenes to ensure they stay there.

This book exists for everyone wishing to enter the broadcasting industry, in whatever job and at whatever level. For it matters not which job you initially aim for in broadcasting, as the chances are you'll end up with a different one. British television presenter and disc jockey Chris Evans was a studio assistant and then a radio producer before making it to the seat behind the microphone and then on to the television screen; many television and radio sports commentators were sporting stars first – Ian Botham and Sue Barker, for example. Many actors, writers or presenters become producers – John Cleese, Jonathan Ross; many writers end up fronting their own programmes – Melvyn Bragg, Ben Elton.

What this book will do is inform you what the many jobs in broadcasting are and, as important, how they inter-link with each other. It will also explain the possible career paths – and make it clear where and when those paths are likely to end or turn a sharp corner.

This book will also make it clear that most jobs in broadcasting won't make you famous or particularly rich; that extreme wealth and fame are not what broadcasting is all about; and that, often, the jobs can be as rewarding – if not more so – without the extreme wealth and fame.

The many thousands working in the British broadcasting industry staff five national terrestrial television stations, 23 BBC and independent regional stations, around 90 cable and satellite television services, eight BBC and independent national terrestrial radio stations, 38 BBC local radio stations, 157 independent local radio stations, 14 satellite radio stations and nine cable radio stations.

The number of people working in the British broadcasting industry is almost impossible to calculate because over 60 per cent of them are freelance and there is now no union closed shop, so the number of BECTU members – around 30,000 – is not an effective guide. But those 30,000, and the many others who are not union members, include everyone from electricians to musicians; from producers to presenters; from make-up artists to set designers; from accountants to lawyers; from studio hands to continuity announcers and from newsreaders to script editors. The extremely rich and famous make up a fraction of Britain's broadcasting workforce, and most of them started in exactly the same way as you – with enthusiasm, a passion for broadcasting, but struggling to know the best way to adapt your talents to it.

This book will help you with that struggle. Maintaining the enthusiasm or passion, on the other hand, is entirely up to you.

2

BROADCASTING: THE BACKGROUND

SO MUCH HAS CHANGED

Almost daily, the media bring into sharp focus the communications revolution we have experienced in recent years, are experiencing today, and will continue to experience for some time. Everywhere we look and listen, we are reminded of the information technology explosion which has touched the lives of everyone living in the 1990s.

For example: it wasn't long ago that *The Sunday Times* was little more than just another daily newspaper with a colour magazine thrown in as a weekend treat. Today, that Sunday paper, like many others in the UK, is now thicker than a week's worth of its daily sister paper put together. New technology and the weakening of the print unions are the principal causes of that.

For another example: in most parts of the UK, you can now receive five national BBC radio channels, at least one local BBC radio channel, the BBC's World Service, two or three national independent radio channels and a handful of community radio channels. New – and cheaper – broadcasting technology, the deregulation of the airwaves and the weakening of the broadcasting unions are the principal causes of that.

And for another example: the minimum number of terrestrial television channels you can receive in the UK today is five; you might also be able to receive a further 20–30 cable and/or satellite channels, depending upon how well-wired you are; and you probably have at least one VCR and maybe a multimedia PC with CD-ROM or Video CD drive – and/or a CD-I player. The reasons for this increased availability of audiovisual entertainment in the home are the relaxation of broadcasting regulations, new – and

4

cheaper – technology, and the weakening of the broadcasting and artists' unions.

And it's important to note how recent these changes are. Only seven years ago there was no satellite television in the UK; 15 years ago there was no Channel 4; 25 years ago there was no independent (non-state-run) radio in the UK; 30 years ago there was no BBC2; and 42 years ago there was no independent television in the UK – and the only television channel available was broadcast by the BBC – the channel now known as BBC1.

Twenty years ago there were almost no domestic VCRs. Six years ago there was no CD-I and only two years ago was the technology sufficient to enable video (full-motion video) to be encoded on to CD-ROM disks. The world's big electronics companies have only just decided on the standard for the new films-on-CD format, or digital video disc (DVD).

SO MUCH HAS CHANGED – SO MUCH REMAINS THE SAME

Yes, there's more television, radio and newsprint out there than ever before, but how much of what we see and hear is very different from the early days?

In *Back to the Future II*, Steven Spielberg presents us with a nightmare scenario where, in the year 2015, a young man watching a seemingly still image of flowers, trees and fields on a wall-mounted screen is reminded by a television presenter that 'You are tuned to The Scenery Channel.'

Spielberg's vision of the future (that film was made in 1985) was frighteningly accurate. Multichannel technology has moved so fast that broadcasters today find it increasingly difficult to fill the ever-growing number of channels. Today, it seems almost as though the channels come first, and then we try to find something to fill them with – a reason for their existence. To use Marshall McLuhan's well-worn observation of 1962, *the medium is the message*. ('The Medium Is The Message' is the much-quoted title of Chapter 1 of the book *Understanding Media* (1964) by Marshall McLuhan.) No longer is it enough to be guided by a simple maxim such as that used by John Charles Walsham Reith, 1st Baron Reith of Stonehaven (better known as plain Lord Reith – appointed the first general manager of the BBC back in 1922, and director-general between 1927 and 1938), who decreed that the primary goal of all the Corporation's output was 'to inform, educate and entertain'. Today, most channel bosses would love to be guided only by those Reithian objectives. The problem is, they now have others to add to the list, like: fill the airtime on a limited budget; win a bigger audience than the ever-growing opposition; provide programming which pleases the advertisers and sponsors; make sure the channel gets regular publicity in the tabloid press; and provide a reasonable return to the shareholders.

THE BROADCASTING ACT 1990

In November 1990, the Broadcasting Act 1990 received royal assent. This Act, inextricably linked to the then prime minister Margaret Thatcher, changed the face of British broadcasting for ever – at least, it changed the structure of the industry for ever, if not for better. In brief, the Act forced the auctioning of the ITV companies to the highest bidder. This sent damaging shock waves through the industry as companies had to shed jobs and cut production in order to remain in operation. The subsequent change in ownership rules also meant that today far fewer people own and run ITV than before the Act; in effect it has become a less democratic organisation, with power – and resulting wealth – concentrated into far fewer hands.

The Act also paved the way for satellite and cable in the UK, and Channel 5. It also introduced the law stipulating that both ITV and the BBC should commission at least 25 per cent of their productions from independent producers. The television business in the UK was never the same again.

BUT HOW DIFFERENT ARE THE PROGRAMMES?

Yes, the media landscape has changed radically. But so much of radio and television's output hasn't. Television newsreaders in the UK still wear suits and, if male (and most still are), ties. Only since the arrival of Channel 4's live weekday morning show *The Big Breakfast* in 1993 have we seen newsreaders in shirt sleeves. Most newsreaders in the UK, still, are white and pronounce with middle-class accents.

The top-rated programmes are still costume dramas, news bulletins and soap operas. In 1995, the most-watched television drama series was the BBC's adaptation of Jane Austen's *Pride and Prejudice* which captured the public imagination, regularly topping the ratings and making the headlines. Almost 30 years ago, back in the late 1960s, the BBC's adaptation of John Galsworthy's *The Forsyte Saga* similarly captured the hearts – and the headlines – of the nation.

Much current affairs programming today relies on formulae established in the early years of broadcasting; many documentaries still echo the styles and techniques developed by the great pre-television documentary film makers of the 1930s and 1940s like John Grierson and Lindsay Anderson. It is a paradox that while television and radio have been at the heart of a continuing communications revolution which has enabled live and pre-recorded sound and images to be beamed instantly into pretty well every home in every country in the civilised world, their output has always been restricted by, in television's case, the size of the screen and the time limit imposed on a given broadcast; and in radio's case, the inability to project images and, again, time limits.

To expand, fairly early on in the evolution of television and radio, the die was cast. In the interests of variety, budget and the limited attention span of the average person, a number of general – and often unwritten – rules were established from the very beginning, for example:

- That a one-off television drama should rarely last longer than 90 minutes – 115 at the most.
- That the episodes of a television drama series should generally last between 45 and 55 minutes.
- That the episodes of a television comedy series/soap opera should – other than in exceptional circumstances – last around 25 minutes.
- That a television news broadcast should last around 15 minutes – or 25–30 minutes if shown in peak time.
- That (almost) all radio stations should broadcast news and weather bulletins hourly or half-hourly.
- That music radio should be punctuated with talk, news, announcements and the occasional discussion.

These and other long-established 'rules' still apply, in spite of the many technological changes which have occurred.

The ways in which such rules came about are complex. Drama

was always restricted by studio space or, in the case of exterior shots, travel, cost, light and weather. News bulletins have always been determined by a number of elements, not least how much 'real' news there is around in any given day; how quickly it can be reported and verified; and how, in the case of television, it can be represented visually. Comedy works best in short bursts – hence the fact that most sitcoms are never longer than 25 minutes, and the development of the short comedy sketch.

Much of radio output is determined by the movements of its audience on any given day. Unlike television, which knows that, in general, its audience is sitting down, watching and listening to that which comes out of the box in the corner and doing little else, radio has to plan for an audience which may be cooking, driving, dozing in bed, reading, working in an office or factory, sitting in a hairdressing salon or, more recently, jogging while plugged into a personal stereo. Hence the development of such radio concepts as the 'drive-time' hours at the beginning and end of each weekday; the 'after the kids (and husband?) have gone to school/work discussion programme' after 9 a.m.; the lunchtime news (when the male listenership increases again); and the afternoon play. Hence, too, the crucial 'breakfast show', which, in both talk and music radio, is where most of the money is invested. Grab your listeners first thing in the morning – when most people are doing their own thing and speaking very little to anyone else – and you've got them for life. Or so the theory goes.

Genres and styles in radio and television differ from country to country, but much of the look or sound of any given country's television and radio was similarly culturally or socially determined pretty early on in the evolution of broadcasting.

American television has always looked different from British television. The Americans have always liked their car chases, while the British have always preferred their dramas in the drawing room. This can be put down to the fact that American television has its roots in sunny Hollywood, the country's film capital, chosen for its year-round sunshine (hence lots of light and warmth for outdoor filming), while British television has its roots in its highly prized theatre – and to some extent, in radio.

GETTING WORK IN BROADCASTING

So, with all the technological advances which are changing and expanding the broadcasting industry worldwide, what of the jobs available? Does the growth in satellite and cable and new video formats mean more jobs? Well, look at the new channels that have been launched in recent years – for example the UK's retro-cult channel Bravo (showing predominantly old series) and American broadcasting mogul Ted Turner's TNT/Cartoon Channel (showing Hanna–Barbera cartoons and old MGM movies). In the case of these two channels, most of the programmes have already been made, so any new jobs will be in the transmission or management areas, rather than on the typically more attractive production side.

The production sector of the industry has not grown as fast as those sectors which have had to sustain its growth through new technology – primarily the business side of the industry – although deregulation and a change in the role of the unions have made some of broadcasting's more creative jobs more accessible. Many still complain that, in the UK particularly, it's who you know rather than what you know that will get you into this business. Occasional surveys continue to reveal a high proportion of graduates from Oxford and Cambridge working at the BBC, and establishing a more realistic racial mix among broadcasting staff at both radio and television stations throughout the UK continues to prove difficult.

Sex discrimination remains a problem too. Camera operators are still more often referred to as cameramen. This is because, in the early days film and television camera equipment was big and heavy and traditionally the operation of heavy machinery has always been entrusted to men. Television directors, too, have almost always been male, while production assistants – with their eternal calm and extraordinary organisational skills (see chapter 11) have traditionally always been women. Things are changing, but not quickly, and the sexual divides in broadcasting will be dealt with again elsewhere in this book.

AN OVER-CROWDED PROFESSION

The most persistent problem facing those wishing to work in broadcasting, however, is that it appeals to so many people. The work is exciting, whether you're behind the scenes or in the public eye. Therefore, every job advertised – and even those which aren't – is always heavily over-subscribed. This makes the job of selecting the right person extremely difficult.

This is where word-of-mouth comes into play. Recommendation of a person by a trusted employee is a gift to an employer, and hence so many positions in broadcasting are still filled via the grapevine – whether the jobs are advertised or not. I have held numerous positions in radio and television and all but one came by word-of-mouth.

The situation is changing as more media courses come into being (see appendix A), as they can bring to employers' attention those people who are showing particular flair or enthusiam in specific areas.

The situation is changing, also, as the media generally expand and cross-fertilise. The 1980s explosion in style magazines, for example (*The Face, I-D,* etc.), brought a number of young people to the attention of radio and television producers, and hence a new wave of young music, style and fashion journalists went on to become radio and television personalities. Television and radio star Danny Baker started his media life as founder-editor of punk magazine *Sniffin' Glue*; presenter of the BBC's *Clothes Show* Caryn Franklin, as a former student at St Martin's College of Art, went on first to write for street-style and music magazine *I-D*; former editor of *Smash Hits* David Hepworth went on to present the BBC's *Old Grey Whistle Test* and a rock show for the BBC's London radio station GLR; the editor of satirical magazine *Private Eye*, Ian Hislop, is now involved in a number of news and satire-related television programmes, notably BBC2's *Have I Got News For You?* – and they are the well-known names. Many other newspaper and magazine people now move to radio and television behind-the-scenes jobs, for example as news reporters, researchers and producers.

On the technical side, too, courses are springing up all over the place on which you can learn film, video and radio production (see appendix A). Such courses were rare 20 years ago as the equipment required was bulky and expensive. Technological developments, however, have now made such courses easier to run and so more people can now learn technical broadcasting skills away from the workplace rather than on-the-job, as was necessary in the early days of broadcasting.

One can also teach oneself rudimentary technical skills in the privacy of one's own home, as the cost of camcorders and other related equipment continues to plummet. Note that if you're aiming for the creative side of television or radio, prospective employers will always be impressed to see or hear your own work, whatever the conditions in which it was made.

YOU'LL BE IN GOOD COMPANY

As you move on through this book to read about the jobs and how to set about getting them, bear in mind the size of this industry – 30,000 official union members and an incalculable number of others – and how everyone's job links somewhere and somehow with everyone else's. It's important to have an overview of the industry and to understand what everyone else is doing and how they got where they are.

Read on and this book might help you decide whether, where and how you might fit into this giant jigsaw puzzle.

3

RADIO: PAST AND PRESENT

HOW IT ALL BEGAN

With television now playing such a prominent role in all of our lives, it is easy to forget that the birth of broadcasting happened with the birth of radio. Radio recently celebrated its 100th anniversary (1995). For the sake of history, it is worth briefly looking back 100 years to remind ourselves of exactly what happened.

THE BIRTH OF RADIO – THE BIRTH OF BROADCASTING

In 1888, experiments carried out by German physicist Heinrich Hertz confirmed the theory put forward by Scottish physicist James Clerk Maxwell some 14 years before, that electromagnetic energy can travel as waves. Hertz's name was later given to the unit of frequency used to measure these radio waves, although the first waves weren't sent until a successful experiment by Italian engineer and inventor Guglielmo Marconi in 1895. Marconi patented the Hertzian wave for use in telegraphic communication one year later, and in 1897 formed the Wireless Telegraph and Signal Company, the world's first radio hardware company, later to become known as the Marconi Co.

It was to be over 20 years before regular radio broadcasts, as we know them today, would start. Between 1919 and 1921 experimental stations went on air in Europe, and local stations began broadcasting in the US. In 1922, regular broadcasts began in Moscow; the French began transmitting from the Eiffel Tower; and on November 14 of that year, the British Broadcasting Corporation (BBC) broadcast the world's first ever national radio programme across the UK, signalling the launch of a schedule of regular broadcasts which would fast make it the most revered and respected broadcasting organisation in the world.

It was also in 1922 that radio got its first royalty demands – from the American Society of Composers, Authors and Publishers, now better known as ASCAP, which collects performing rights payments and licence fees for artists and composers; the British equivalent is the PRS or Performing Rights Society. In the early days, as now, radio programmers found music – pre-recorded or live – to be both popular with audiences and easy to programme. They also saw music as a very cheap means of filling broadcast time. But ASCAP soon put paid to that, and music today has become one of the most expensive elements in what is otherwise a relatively cheap form of broadcasting when compared with television.

RADIO'S COMING OF AGE

Many talk of 'the three ages of radio'. The first lasted from the early 1920s through to the mid-1950s, when the BBC first started broadcasting on FM – or perhaps the 1960s, when, in Britain in particular, radio 'pirates' began the lengthy struggle to open up the airwaves.

Then came a period of expansion beginning in the UK with the launch of Radio 1, the BBC's answer to the now-outlawed pirates – many of whom, ironically, staffed the new pop station – and ending with the establishment of community radio, which followed the introduction of local, followed by national, independent advertiser-funded stations.

And the third age begins somewhere in the early-to-mid-1990s, with Digital Audio Broadcasting (DAB) putting the fear of God into the music industry – those people whom ASCAP, PRS and others have been 'protecting' from radio since its outset – because of the prospect of consumers being able to record pristine digital broadcasts of its music via DAB channels, and thus stopping buying its records for ever.

Well, DAB probably won't destroy the music industry, just as the pirates didn't and Marconi didn't before them. But the fact that radio is still frightening people – for whatever reason – is a testament to its power. It may be television's poor relation in the minds of some, but it's growing today as fast as it ever did and, free from the confines of that oblong screen permanently stuck in the corner of the room, is still the world's most accessible and versatile means of communication.

THE BBC

In the UK, it was the BBC that set the mould. It began broadcasting nationally in 1922 under the regime of Lord Reith, who ran the Corporation like a ship and stuck religiously to two guiding principles: that the BBC was a public service and its output should be guided accordingly (see previous chapter), and that it should be an independent voice, untampered with by government or commerce.

His determination to protect the latter principle was beautifully illustrated when, during the general strike of 1926, the then Chancellor of the Exchequer Winston Churchill – who became prime minister in 1940 after the outbreak of the Second World War – suggested that the government take over the BBC during this national emergency because its broadcasts were not always toeing the government line. Believing religiously in the Corporation's true independence, Reith held out against Churchill, bolstered partly by his friendship with the then prime minister Stanley Baldwin. But from then began a continual battle between successive governments and the BBC, the former regularly accusing the BBC of anti-government bias and the latter regularly accusing the government of attempting to use the Corporation as a pro-government mouthpiece or of imposing censorship by the back door. And this battle still rages . . .

THE REITHIAN LEGACY

Lord Reith's 'inform, educate and entertain' maxim remains largely intact even today. The recent history of the BBC has been somewhat tarnished by often vicious internal and external debate as to how, or whether, it should 'modernise' to survive alongside a private sector which has been alternately expanding and then buying itself up as regulations affecting the broadcasting industry as a whole continue to change.

Nonetheless, the style and production values established in the early days of BBC Radio's Home Service, Light Programme and Third Programme (later, in radio's second age, to become Radio

4, Radio 2 and Radio 3 respectively when Radio 1 came into being in September 1967) are still revered, respected and much copied.

Interestingly, when new or established radio stations in the UK do attempt to deviate from the norm – the BBC way of doing things – they rarely succeed. A good case in point is Talk Radio, the first national rival to the BBC's talk station Radio 4, which was launched in early 1995. It promised controversy via its 'shock jocks' (an abbreviation for shocking disc jockeys), a concept borrowed from the United States, where the best-known exponent of this intentionally vulgar style of radio broadcasting is Howard Stern.

Talk Radio was clearly trying to do something different. Prior to its existence, the only other successful talk service in the UK was the London independent station best known as LBC (various management and ownership changes saw its name change from London Broadcasting – or LBC – to London News Radio, then to London Radio, and then back to LBC in the space of seven years between 1989 and 1996). LBC introduced a number of new ideas to differentiate it from the BBC's all-talk service Radio 4 – notably the daily live phone-in. But in essence it succeeded by sounding like a faster, more popular version of Radio 4, with advertisements. In its early days, for example, LBC's flagship morning programme *AM* was presented by Bob Holness and Douglas Cameron, two former presenters of Radio 4's flagship morning programme, *Today*.

Talk Radio's radical new approach failed, and within a year, a decision was made to get rid of the shock jocks and, effectively, create a national version of LBC – which has always been, effectively, a commercial version of Radio 4.

It's interesting to note, too, that during a period in the late 1980s and early 1990s, under Australian management, LBC attempted to bring some of the brash Australian broadcasting style so successful down under to the London airwaves – to the extent of bringing Australian presenter Mike Carlton over to host its breakfast show. A star in his home country, Carlton nonetheless failed to boost LBC's ratings in the UK. And it was, once again, back to the British – or the BBC – way.

THE PIRATES

This idea that the BBC set the mould which can never be broken, certainly in the UK, can be misread as reactionary conservatism. The point, however, is rather that the huge resources and mono-poly position the BBC enjoyed for so many years as the world's first state-run broadcasting corporation allowed it to develop free from commercial pressures and to build a highly trained and experienced workforce. Its public-service ethos, as fiercely guarded by Lord Reith, gave it a reputation for intelligent, accu-rate and unbiased reporting which won it respect among the most influential people in the country – even the establishment. It has thus become part of the fabric of the United Kingdom and there-fore any proposed radical change in, or threats to, its structure or output are taken most seriously: the radio pirates, for example.

The radio pirates were a phenomenon of Britain in the 1960s and, like so much of that era – during which Britain seemed to rule the world in all things popular, from the Mini car to the Beatles and from fashion to football – are today remembered fondly, in spite of the fact that they were all breaking at least British civil law.

They came into being, essentially, because the British govern-ment was tightly limiting the airwaves, allowing only the BBC to broadcast. Meanwhile, British and American pop music had become an essential element of youth culture not only in the UK and America but in many other parts of the world too. Yet there was no proper outlet for it via the UK's highly regarded broadcasting corporation except through a handful of specialist programmes and Radio Luxembourg, a commercial pop channel whose broadcasts from the Grand Duchy were powerful enough to reach the UK. What the British audiences wanted was a non-stop pop music station, like those which were starting up in the United States. The BBC, heavily guarded by the establishment, wouldn't provide it – the government effectively forbade anyone else to broadcast – so a group of young people got together and found a way around British law that would enable them to broad-cast non-stop pop across the UK.

The loophole in the law they discovered was based around what became known as the three-mile limit – the distance from the coast of the UK after which people were not subject to civil law. The pirates decided that if they were to broadcast from ships anchored outside the three-mile limit, then they couldn't be touched.

The two best-known pirate stations were Radio London and Radio Caroline, both run from ships off the coast of Britain. Pirate disc jockeys included Tony Blackburn, Noel Edmunds, Johnny Walker and the late Kenny Everett, all but the last still active and well known in the media today.

Needless to say, neither the government nor the BBC was particularly fond of the pirates; the music industry, too, complained that the pirates were playing its music without paying royalties. The pirates said they would pay those royalties, and pay for the right to broadcast, if the government would grant them licences – through what was then known as the Ministry of Posts and Telecommunications headed by Tony Benn, then Postmaster General.

The government refused, and at the same time closed the three-mile limit loophole to the point at which the pirates were eventually, in 1967, forced to shore. They were pardoned, and many of them were re-employed by the BBC's new all-pop music station Radio 1. The station's first programme was broadcast on September 30, 1967 – its presenter was Tony Blackburn.

THE BBC LOSES ITS MONOPOLY

So the government had beaten the pirates, and the BBC had brought them into its fold. The launch of Radio 1 in 1967 saw the start of the modernisation of the BBC, with its other stations renamed Radios Two, Three and Four. There followed a period of fierce debate between the BBC – whose proposals for change were put forward in a document entitled *Broadcasting in the Seventies* – and The Campaign for Better Broadcasting, which was set up directly to resist the BBC's document and was fronted by a number of celebrities including Dr Jonathan Miller, George Melly and Henry Moore.

The debate was long and complicated. This radical look at the BBC did result in big changes in the early 1970s which included the abolition of the radio-only licence (the television licence would finance all BBC operations from then onwards), the ending of the Post Office's control of broadcasting hours and the passing of responsibility for broadcasting in the UK from the Ministry of Posts and Telecommunications to the Home Office.

Significant to the listener in the early 1970s was the growth in the number of BBC local radio stations, which numbered one – Radio Leicester – in 1967 and 20 by November 1973. Also significant to the listener was the Sound Broadcasting Act of 1972, which gave the go-ahead for independent local radio (ILR) in the UK, which would be supervised by the ITA (see chapter 7). The first ILR station LBC (London Broadcasting), an all-talk and news station, was finally launched in 1973 with its sister station Capital Radio, a pop station to rival Radio 1 in London, following one year later.

THE 1990S

BBC Radio got its fifth channel finally in 1990, when in August of that year Radio 5 was launched with a package of education, youth and sports programmes. It suffered much criticism and after four years on the air was relaunched as all-news and sports channel, Five Live. At around the same time came the relaunch of Radio 1, which itself drew fierce criticism when, under the management of Matthew Bannister, a former ILR man, many of the channel's 'old guard' DJs were got rid of.

But the early 1990s were a period of panic for the BBC, for these were the years leading up to the renewal of the Corporation's charter in 1996. The Corporation's management feared the worst, particularly given the radical changes imposed on ITV by the 1990 Broadcasting Act. But by and large the charter has been renewed until the year 2006 year with the Corporation's status as a state-funded broadcasting service financed by the licence fee intact.

THE FUTURE

The future, though, will become less and less dominated by the BBC. There are now three national independent radio stations in the UK: Classic FM, Talk Radio and Virgin Radio; and here is an example of just how much local radio activity there is across the UK: in its first four years since it took over the role of regulating independent radio licences from the IBA in 1991 (see chapter 7), the Radio Authority has awarded the above three national licences and 52 new local radio licenses; and has re-advertised over 120 existing licences.

Local radio, cable and satellite radio, and even radio over the Internet, are between them increasingly eating into the BBC's audience share. I will, however, be referring to the BBC as a model throughout this book, as it remains the best-staffed, best-resourced and most highly regarded radio service in the UK and probably the world.

4

RADIO: THE PEOPLE

Radio is all about people.

When we think of the famous people in the world of broadcasting we tend to think of television personalities – the faces we see on the screen and which cause us to double-take on those rare occasions when we see them in the street, in a restaurant or in an airport lounge. Yet there's so much more than people on television; there's music; there's nature – landscapes and wild animals; there are cartoons and puppets; there are pop videos; there's news footage; there are advertisements; there are test cards, credits at the end of the programmes and inventive graphics at the beginning.

But on radio there are only people – and only their voices at that. And there's music. But we'll come to that later.

TALK RADIO

It's quite amazing that it's possible to broadcast talk 24 hours a day, keep the programmes varied, hardly ever repeat anything, and come up with something new to say, hour after hour, day after day – and keep the listeners' attention. But it is possible. It's difficult, but it's possible.

That it is difficult has been proved by the two independent talk stations which have been launched in the UK in the last 30 years: London Broadcasting – which was originally known as LBC and which between 1990 and 1996 went through a number of ownership and name changes only to end up once again as LBC (and which during its troubled existence has nearly gone bust several times); and the national, independent Talk Radio, which in its first two years between 1994 and 1996 went through one ownership change and three editorial relaunches.

What is difficult about talk radio is that it's labour-intensive and therefore costly; and it is generally regarded as minority programming. As such it has to walk a fine line between an intelligent editorial approach (so that at least it's listened to by opinion makers, and therefore can offer prestige value rather than large audiences to advertisers) and popularity. Being listened to by the nation's opinion makers is fine as long as you have other listeners as well; audience figures which drop too low will put off even the most exclusive of advertisers as well as call into question whether or not the station is fulfilling the terms of its licence.

State-run talk radio – in the UK that's Radio 4 and Radio 5 – has an easier time of it because its income is guaranteed via the licence fee, and therefore it is better resourced and so can spend more money and time finding that balance between intelligent editorial approach and popularity. An example of how Radio 4 does this can be found in the contrast between its highly regarded morning news show *Today* (which is listened to by pretty well every British member of parliament, political commentators, captains of industry, community and church leaders – not to mention many thousands of people like you and me) and its hugely popular and long-running soap opera *The Archers*. Both are expensive to produce, but together they serve to give the station a very strong identity – one of authority (as reinforced by *AM*) but also one of home-spun charm and humour (as reinforced by *The Archers*). In the absence of music, the establishment of such an identity is crucial. But it takes time and resources – and therefore money – to do this, and that is why Radio 4's independent rivals have had such a tough time of it, particularly against such well-established competition.

TALK RADIO: A DAY IN THE LIFE

If you were lucky enough to get a staff position or a long-term freelance contract with a talk radio station, the likelihood is that you would be assigned to a particular programme rather than the station as a whole. This is the easiest way in which to run a talk radio station – any radio station, in fact, as it simply involves dividing up the day into programme times. A different production team – including presenters and reporters – is assigned to fill each designated time, usually with a named programme. So, a fictitious talk radio station might begin with a three-hour news programme from 7 a.m. to 10 a.m., followed by a two-hour phone-in programme until 12 noon, and a midday news hour until 1 p.m. From 1 p.m. to 3 p.m. there might be a slightly lighter approach to programming, featuring consumer, home and health items, personality interviews and so on, and from 3 p.m. to 5 p.m., an arts programme. From 5 p.m. to 7 p.m. there might be news again, followed by a drama or a quiz show. Evening and overnight programming might once again be phone-ins or digests of the day's news and other events; in the case of the BBC's Radio 4, the station shuts down between 1 a.m. and 5.55 a.m. All but the drama and the quiz show would probably be live, although all the programme slots would include pre-recorded interviews and other reports.

If you were assigned, say, to the 3 p.m. to 5 p.m. slot as a researcher or programme assistant, for example, your day might begin at around 10 a.m., when you would be in the office looking through the day's newspapers and the week's magazines, in search of stories which you might be able to follow up for your programme. The newspapers might, on that day, be full of stories about the break-up of a long-lasting showbusiness marriage. For the purposes of your programme this could become an item – even a discussion – on the pressures showbusiness puts on a marriage. Potential guests would be hurriedly phoned (either to appear live on the programme or to make a live or pre-recorded contribution by phone), old newspaper cuttings would be gathered from the station's cuttings library, and even old tapes might be trawled to find quotes from past interviews which might be relevant to the issue.

The marriage-and-showbusiness item might last 12–15 minutes if it can become a studio discussion; otherwise rather less. So there is still much time to fill. There will be interviews which may have been recorded earlier in the week which will require editing to fill a slot; there will be other guests due to come in to talk about their latest book, film or recipe – or to give advice on a certain pre-arranged topic of the day. There will also be reports put together by the programme's reporters: one might yesterday have attended the star-studded opening of a new restaurant; another might have spent the day with a group of people who are protesting about the building of a road through a particular piece of countryside.

The reporters behind these stories will probably be assigned full-time to the programme in question and will be out getting their stories either under specific orders from the programme's producer, or from their own ideas put to the producer, perhaps during a production meeting. They might spend half a day getting their reports out 'on location', making notes and recording interviews and other bits of sound for 'atmosphere'; and then they will be back in the studio, cutting the tape and writing short paragraphs which they will record in the studio and edit into the report as it builds. This report will then be handed to the producer on tape, along with a piece of paper on which will be written the 'in' and the 'out' cues – in other words, the report's opening and closing words, plus exactly how long the report lasts. The reporter might also write an introduction or 'intro' to the piece for the presenter to read out on air before the report is played.

And this is just one programme. Throughout the radio station little production teams sat around clusters of desks (with some members occasionally running along to a studio to record something or cut a piece of tape) will be similarly putting their programme together in order to be able to fill their particular time slot. Working with these people will be several levels of management which will be deciding programming policy and staffing policy, along with sales and marketing policy. There will also be a small engineering staff whose job essentially will be to keep the technical side going.

INDEPENDENT TALK RADIO: THE STAFFING STRUCTURE

At the top there will be a chairman. He or she will from day to day have little to do with the running of the station; the chairman's name will be on the letterhead, and this person might from time to time provide the public face of the station – in news interviews and so on. Otherwise this is a person you'll rarely meet.

Next will probably be the managing director (MD), who again won't be too involved in the day-to-day running of the station, certainly as far as the programmes are concerned. What the MD will be doing, however, will be running the business: working alongside the finance director and the board to establish and maintain a long-term business plan for the station. As far as the producers, the presenters and the engineers are concerned, the MD will not play a significant role in their lives, unless major policy changes need to be implemented or, as happens increasingly frequently, a redundancy programme.

Next there might be an editorial director, whose job it would be to establish editorial policy. Working directly to the editorial director will be the programme controller, who will deal with day-to-day programming issues and implement editorial policy. The programme controller might appoint producers, co-ordinate the programme schedules under instructions from the editorial director, and play a key organisational role at times when temporary schedule changes are required – during a general election, for example, or at holiday periods such as Christmas. Producers with particularly difficult staffing or editorial decisions to make might refer upwards to the programme controller in certain circumstances.

Under the programme controller there may be a deputy programme controller, who will, of course, deputise in the absence of the programme controller, take on some of the more arduous administration of the station, and even produce a regular programme.

THE PRODUCTION TEAM

Then come the people who actually make the programmes: the producer, the programme assistant (or studio assistant – see next chapter) and the presenter or presenters. On most independent stations this is about as much of a production team as you'd get. There might be a studio engineer to operate the desk (fade up microphones, fade in music, etc.) but in the new lean and mean days of radio this will be done either by the producer or by the presenter – in which case the presenter will be 'self-opping' (operating the equipment him or herself). At the BBC, on the other hand, most programmes will have a bigger staff – including studio assistants, researchers and even assistant producers. Above the producer in both the independent talk station and at the BBC there might be a sequence editor or series editor who is in charge of a particular 'day part' or series and will oversee the week's programming relating to that series or day part rather

than working on a programme-by-programme basis as the producer would. The sequence editor would be above the producer
in the hierarchy.

INDEPENDENT MUSIC RADIO: THE STAFFING STRUCTURE

In the case of an independent music radio station, the chairman
and managing director will perform similar roles to those outlined
above. The editorial director might be known as the 'station
manager' in case of a music station, and below this person might
be the programme controller.

Again after that it's down to the individual producers to craft
their programmes to suit, and to fit, the day's and week's schedules, but of course as with a music station most of a programme's
content is music – which mainly comes from discs provided to the
station by record companies or taken from the station's library –
less research and general programme planning are required than
for a talk station.

In a large radio station like Radio 1, it is the producer who
has the greatest say over what gets played, and will fashion the
playlist of his or her particular show according to the presenter's
style and the *house playlist* – the list of records which can and
can't be played for various reasons – which is decided upon
weekly at a meeting.

On all but a very few independent stations, radio playlists (the
schedule of titles which are played across the station's output in
any given week) are put together by off-the-shelf computer pro-
grams. New titles with accompanying identifying information are
fed into the computer on a weekly basis, and the computer then
works out what should be played and when. So in such cases
even the individual programme producer won't necessarily have
any say over what records are included in his or her programme.

Music stations will have their own news programmes and the
occasional documentary; there will also be star interviews and
other items of interest which don't involve the straight playing
of music. On larger music stations these programmes will be
researched and produced in-house by a production team, just as
programmes on a talk radio station would be – unless an independent producer is commissioned to make them. Smaller music
stations would generally use on-the-hour news bulletins provided

by an outside news service such as IRN (see chapter 6) rather than make their own news programmes.

Whereas with a talk radio station the main expense is staff and news sources – people to make and voice the programmes, along with any news wire services which might be subscribed to – with a music station the main expense is the music, which is paid for in the form of PRS returns. PRS stands for Performing Rights Society, a body which collects royalties on behalf of its member musicians and artists. Every record which is played on any radio station – or on television for that matter – must be logged, with information including the record label, the publisher, the artist and how many seconds of the record was played. This logged information is then passed on to the PRS, which will in turn bill the radio station for the amount of music played and pay the respective artists (minus a collecting fee) accordingly.

INDEPENDENT PRODUCTIONS

As well as the station-based production teams busy working day in, day out to prepare their programmes on time, there will be a handful of independent production companies producing programmes on behalf of the station.

The independent radio production sector is nowhere near as big as television's equivalent, but it is a small thriving sector nonetheless. There is considerable overlap between the two media in fact; Chris Evans' Ginger Productions, which produced his Channel 4 entertainment programme *Don't Forget Your Toothbrush* and his Friday night show *TFI Friday*, also produces his BBC Radio 1 breakfast show. There are several cases of radio presenters owning the production company which makes the programme they present. Here you have the rather bizarre situation in which an independent production company uses station facilities (which it hires from the station), operates under station regulations, and works alongside station employees. The station in this case pays none of the presenters or production staff but instead pays a flat fee for the programme.

Having looked at a few types of radio station and the way in which the people interact through the structure of the station, we will move on to look at some of the jobs in more detail.

5

RADIO: THE JOBS

Having discussed the structure of a radio station and the way in which management and production staff interact, we will now take a look at a number of the jobs available in radio and how you might set about getting them.

THE PRODUCER

The radio producer's job will vary widely depending upon the type of programme in question. The producer's role in radio is similar to that of the director in television, in that it is the producer who ultimately determines what the audience will to hear. On a radio documentary the producer will be given a budget and a subject (by the station's programme controller in collaboration with the editorial director, or if the programme is part of a series, the series producer), and will set about staffing the programme with researchers and reporters – the number and calibre depending upon the budget. They will research the programme and bring back information and reports on tape, and this will begin to form the subject of the documentary – augmented by a script written perhaps by the producer or maybe the researcher, depending upon the level of trust between the two and the experience of the researcher. The putting together of the documentary – comprising a voiced script (read by a hired presenter, perhaps, or a station regular), reports, interviews, sound effects and music – will be done by a studio engineer under the direction of the producer. In smaller operations the producer will perhaps do the engineering work.

In a live situation – a live news/magazine programme, for example – the producer will have gathered together scripts beforehand for the presenter to read out at certain points in the programme (written by the producer or a researcher/studio assistant depending upon the level of staffing), along with a number of taped reports and pre-recorded interviews (which again will have been edited by a reporter, or a studio assistant or the producer, depending upon the size of the station and therefore the team). The producer – perhaps with assistance – will also have lined up a number of live guests who will have been booked and scheduled to arrive at a certain time and go on air to be interviewed by the presenter soon afterwards. If there is no studio assistant or researcher on hand, the producer might be the one who has to meet the guests at reception and take them up to the 'green room' (hospitality/waiting room), where they will sit until wanted on air. The producer might also have organised one or two guests (or contributors) to speak on the programme by phone. In such a case a time will have been pre-arranged at which the producer will call the guest and put that guest through to the presenter.

Before the programme the producer will have drawn up a running order which he or she will then endeavour to stick to throughout the programme. In most live programmes this is constantly redrawn (and sometimes dispensed with) as news flashes, late or non-appearing guests and over-running interviews spoil the producer's original intentions.

In music radio the producer's job is much more that of music programmer, choosing the records beforehand (if they're not chosen by computer – see chapter 4), and generally being there for the presenter (or DJ) during the live show. If a particular music radio show involves the odd interview or 'phone out' to a rock star on tour, for example, the producer will also be heavily involved in both the planning and the execution of this. In music radio the producer will also ultimately be responsible for the PRS returns (see chapter 4), although if there is a studio assistant or an assistant producer this will very likely be delegated downwards.

In summary, the producer is in charge. There are radio programmes in which the presenter is such a 'star', such a well-known and highly prized personality, that he or she might take elements of the producer's role as and when he or she feels like it. This is often something the producer has to put up with, because inevitably it will involve the presenter making certain decisions from behind the microphone without actually having to do the legwork – which the producer will be expected to do. In such situations, the producer has to respect the presenter's wishes, and get the job done without resenting that presenter. The best programmes are those where the producer and presenter have a rapport and a mutual respect, where the presenter makes occasional creative and constructive suggestions, but where ultimately the producer is firmly in control.

THE PRODUCER: GETTING THE JOB

Many will agree that it's the best job in radio. You shape the programme, but you don't have to put your voice and personality into the product. Your goal is a professionally made finished product which the audience enjoys and with which the production team is satisfied. Many college and privately run courses do touch upon radio production, but however well you have learned the job on paper, there is no replacing experience. A producer can start as a studio assistant or researcher (see below), and the really keen would-be producer might well find him or herself fresh out of college and doing one of those jobs unpaid.

The key is to get into a radio station by whatever means and impress the people who matter – without annoying them. Phone operator for a phone-in programme is a job that most radio stations don't want to pay for – yet so many stations are prepared to allow unpaid people to come in and do this actually very important work. Get in this way and impress the people at the station and you're on your way up the ladder, near the top of which stands the producer.

As you will hear time and time again the toughest part is getting in. Once you've done that, all you need to do is prove yourself.

RESEARCHER, PROGRAMME ASSISTANT

The recent history of radio in the UK is one of simultaneous expansion and contraction; expansion of the number of radio stations there are around the country and contraction in the number of staff required to run the average radio station and the average radio programme. So, while a high-rating, mid-morning live phone-in and talk show on a London independent radio station ten years ago might have had a producer, an engineer (to 'drive the desk' – see below), a researcher/ programme assistant, a phone operator and, of course, a presenter, today that programme is likely to have dispensed with the engineer and the phone operator. Replacing those two people would probably be the producer – who would add to his or her duties those of the engineer; and the programme assistant/ researcher – who would also answer the phones.

So the researcher/programme assistant's job becomes something of a mixed bag as production teams become leaner. In the old days of well-staffed production teams this person would, in the case of a daily live news/magazine programme, for example, be setting up guests for the week's programmes, doing odd pieces of research for the producer and the presenter, finding pieces of music which might be required for particular items, checking guests' biographical details, reading the day's newspapers and so on. During the actual live programme the researcher/programme assistant might operate the phone lines if there's a phone-in element to the programme. If he or she is not required in the studio control room during the broadcast then he or she might stay up in the programme office preparing future programmes and remaining on-call in case the producer should require urgent assistance – chasing up a late guest, checking a fact or finding a lost tape or CD, for example.

The BBC's national radio service produces a number of highly informed and often specialist documentary programmes; it also produces weekly programmes dealing with science, religion, politics and other weighty subjects. In such cases researchers will be crucial and might be assigned to programmes because of their particular expertise in a given subject rather than their radio experience. In such a case they might be given radio training in order that they can put their knowledge and experience of their subject to best use at the BBC. Such researchers – who might become known eventually as 'editors' or 'correspondents' in their particular subject (science editor, religious correspondent, etc.) – will be on a considerably higher pay scale than the researcher-cum-studio assistant working on a local radio station.

RESEARCHER, PROGRAMME ASSISTANT: GETTING THE JOB

The situation with this position is similar to that of the producer; you've got to 'get in to get on'. This is a good college-leaver's job, but don't expect it to pay you well – if at all to begin with.

If the course you have done at college or university has a media – even a radio – element to it (see appendix A), then you'll have a head start over others when it came to applying for such a job should one be advertised. But they rarely are. Such jobs often just come out of nowhere: a programme needs an assistant, the producer checks with the accounts department or the programme controller to see if there's enough money for one, and then a friend of the producer or someone from within the station is assigned to the job – possibly on a short-term basis. If one or two students or graduates keen to get into radio have been phoning and writing to that station – or the particular producer in question – asking for work, when this vacancy comes along one of those students or graduates might be the lucky one who gets the job. This is why making yourself known, without making a nuisance of yourself, is so important.

In the case of the science or religious expert who gets work as a researcher on a particular radio documentary or as a correspondent across a number of programmes, journalistic background will be of considerable help in getting such a position. Such jobs at the BBC are often advertised as training positions, but will always require good qualifications in the given subject. To get into the BBC at this sort of training level can mean a prestige job for life. Such jobs are therefore coveted and hard to get.

THE ENGINEER

Again in the 'good old days' even the smallest of independent local radio stations would have had its own engineering team whose jobs would vary from building the studios to installing new equipment to servicing old equipment and 'driving the desks'. The engineers would also dub-off (copy) tapes for producers, set up studio tape recorders in order to record the transmitted programme for the archives, produce carts (pre-recorded cartridges) for the producer or presenter containing jingles or other voiced pieces of information, and generally be around to

31

do any of the fiddly jobs which traditionally producers and researchers didn't have to worry about.

Today, with the exception of the BBC, which has five vast national radio stations to run, most stations will make do with a chief engineer and an engineer's assistant, and many of the tasks listed above will be dealt with by the producer and studio assistant. Meanwhile the chief engineer and assistant will deal with the building of studios, testing out, ordering and installing new equipment, maintaining existing equipment, checking and maintaining links in and out to the transmitter and servicing any other lines in or out of the station.

Engineers used to 'drive the desks' – operate the volume controls for the microphones, play in music, play in pre-recorded items on tape, etc. – but rarely does this happen any more. Instead this job will be done by the programme producer, or in the case of a big-budget programme – a daily live news programme, for example – a studio producer whose work is confined to the programme at hand rather than any long-term preparation. The studio producer functions rather like a television director in a live programme situation – see chapter 10.

THE ENGINEER: GETTING THE JOB

Radio engineers will usually require good education at least to GCSE but usually up to A-level, including a maths or science qualification, a qualification in electronics, and possibly some sort of work experience – as a practising electrician's assistant, for example. The radio engineer will also have to show some interest and experience in radio or some aspect of the media; maybe he or she has built a home recording studio or similar, or worked in hospital or college radio.

Engineering jobs are more likely to be advertised than those for presenters and producers, and job advertisements will often ask for engineers trained to a particular grade (see appendix A).

THE PRESENTER

We all know what the presenter does – because we all hear what the presenter does. But there's a little more to it than that. What's refreshing about radio is that in most stations you will see the presenter – however well known he or she may have become –

sitting at the production desk, sleeves rolled up, in the hours before the programme, typing bits of script, making notes, chatting with producers and researchers just as though he or she is just another member of the team. Which of course he or she is. In radio, the presenter only needs to be a voice; the rest of the person can be scruffily dressed, larking around, running off to the loo or grabbing a cup of coffee during the adverts and news breaks, and the listener need not know anything about it. Such behaviour is not as easy for the television presenter – certainly the live television presenter. So in radio you tend to get a more relaxed type of personality fronting the programmes.

Some presenters get heavily involved in the programme content, while others will just read what's given to them and interview guests as they are told to do by their producers. A presenter must have a good voice, be able to ad-lib without making it sound like an ad-lib, be able to read from a script and make it sound as if he or she is not reading, and generally be able to draw in the listener and hold his or her attention for as long as is necessary.

When not on air the presenter will be involved with programme research, programme policy, and generally looking at the shape of the programme – the content and particularly the scripts – before going on air or into the studio to record. Most presenters will insist on some script changes simply because the words don't suit their way of speaking. Some can change scripts as they are reading them, while others will want to have them rewritten beforehand. A good researcher/producer/scriptwriter will get to know his or her presenter so that such changes are rarely necessary.

The above refers principally to the presenter on the non-music radio station or programme. There are, of course, many more radio DJs than there are pure speech presenters. And the radio DJ's job is a wonderful job. Few will ever tell you otherwise. They play (and keep) all the best – or at least the most popular – of the latest record releases; they often meet the artists; they're wined, dined and flattered by record companies; they can become celebrities, which in turn gives them a further means of making money, *and* they get paid for all this!

Of course, it's not quite as straightforward as that. This is a highly competitive area of work, and it only pays well on BBC Radio 1 and the national Virgin Radio – if you're a well-known name. Local radio DJs (with the exception of those on the very big local stations such as London's Capital Radio) will generally not be that well paid and will usually supplement their income with club work and other personal appearances. That said, it's a job which carries an element of prestige and, to repeat what was said earlier, it's fun to do and there are many in line waiting to do it.

THE PRESENTER: GETTING THE JOB

You don't often see the job advertised, do you? Presenters come to the job in a whole range of different ways. Some might have started their radio career as a radio doctor, a radio DIY expert or even a traffic news announcer from Scotland Yard or the Automobile Association. In such positions they might have made regular appearances on radio as guests on particular programmes and demonstrated their natural ability to speak on the radio, and suddenly, when the next job comes up, they've got it.

Some presenters will have decided that this is the job for them very early on; they might have done a drama or speech training course at college or university, worked on college or hospital radio stations when and wherever possible and touted their 'demo tapes' around for as long as was needed until someone gave them a job. But it doesn't usually work like this. Radio presenters are usually something else first: for example a local newspaper reporter who then joins a local radio station as a news reporter, gets on-air experience, enjoys it and puts him or herself up for every presenter's job that comes along until he or she gets it.

Many producers become presenters; some actors do, as do journalists, writers, comedians and even politicians. If you want to become a presenter above all else in radio you are advised to get in where you can, polish your presenting skills on a hospital radio station or college radio – or even on a tape recorder at home – and build up a portfolio of work, radio experience in any job and, above all, contacts.

On the other hand, the aspiring music radio DJ will have his or her own mobile disco set up at as early an age as possible. With this equipment he or she will get gigs at local discos, weddings and so on. This will earn the aspiring DJ both money and experience. Locally the DJ will make a name for him or herself, whilst keeping in regular touch with a local radio station or two. Eventually a job will become free at one of these stations and if you've done a good enough PR job on yourself, you may stand a chance of getting it.

Alternatively, you will have got yourself a job at your nearest hospital radio station or on college radio. Here you will develop a style – and have the luxury of being able to prepare a tape of your best moments on radio, which you will have duplicated and sent around to every radio station in the country, or at least every radio station you might want to work for.

You may, on the other hand, want to gain your pre-radio experience as a club DJ. This you could do by making such a good name for yourself doing weddings and so on that you're asked to DJ at the local club; by proving, in whatever way, to the club manager that you're right for the place; by starting your own club. As a club DJ, you will begin to serve as a useful indicator to your record suppliers (specialist shops, record companies etc.), of what the club audience is listening to. In such a specialist role you will stand a better chance of getting on-air work once it becomes available, as your name will become known in certain circles which matter.

The getting of a straight music radio DJ's job is as haphazard as that. When you think about it, it always has been. The early DJs were, mainly, pirates (those who were brave enough to risk making illegal broadcasts in order to provide the UK with non-stop music radio unavailable until 1969, when Radio 1 was launched). Some of these are *still* broadcasting now!

There's no law as to what makes a good DJ, and there is no law as to why station bosses and producers choose particular people for the job.

It's tough now – certainly at national level – to get radio DJ work unless you're already famous for something else. Anything else, some may say, other than being a radio DJ! There is always something to be said for working your way up through the small local radio stations (which pay very badly), however. Because even in this increasingly competitive area of the business, talent occasionally does win through.

SALES AND MARKETING

With independent radio, advertising time needs to be sold to keep the station running. This is done by a sales team whose job it is to find businesses and services whose profile might fit that of the station's audience. For this an element of market research is required in order that the sales people can convince their potential customers that advertising on their particular station will help their business.

A radio station will also require people to sell the station itself: 'brand' it with a particular 'profile' or image in order that a certain type of listener (as many as possible) believe it is the station for them. These two jobs – the selling of the advertising air time and the selling of the station itself – are mutually beneficial, as an easily identifiable target audience makes selling advertising easier.

The people who staff the sales and marketing department will be trained in just that – sales and marketing. Radio experience will not always be necessary; it is widely believed in the sales business that if you can sell one thing you can sell anything.

MANAGEMENT

Management posts either come by working your way up through a station or stations – to the post of producer and then upwards to programme controller and then on to editorial director; or they come by appointment from outside. Management in the media is today regarded (perhaps as it should be) as the same as management in any other business. What's needed is experience, a solid and workable business plan and an ability to run an organisation in as profitable a way as possible. A sensibility to the ways of radio would help, although many working in radio today might say that this seems to be a characteristic many managers lack.

For someone coming at management from outside a radio station a good recognised managerial qualification will be essential.

6

RADIO NEWS

For our model in this chapter we will use the BBC Radio news service based in the company's central London headquarters, Broadcasting House. Not because it's typical; in fact it's unique, but the BBC Radio news service is one of the best-resourced in the world and as such provides a perfect model. Most people in the UK with an ambition to work in news radio would aspire to working for the BBC. That's not to decry other services – such as the national independent radio news provider IRN (see appendix B), which warrants respect simply because it provides a good service on a fraction of the money and resources to which the BBC has access.

WHERE THE NEWS COMES FROM

The BBC Radio newsroom gathers information from a wide range of sources. News comes in from the BBC's own network of correspondents around the world; from its network of domestic or regional correspondents, who are constantly working on stories for the BBC's local radio network; from the news wires such as Reuters, AP and PA (see chapter 22); and from the BBC's own wire service, to which the local radio newsrooms provide news.

Gathering this news and sieving through it is a continuous process which goes on 24 hours a day. Initially this job falls to the 'copy tasters', who will be highly trained journalists with a strong news sense. They will be working through the incoming stories, constantly separating the newsworthy from the un-newsworthy. When a story catches their eye, they will immediately alert one of the duty news editors.

At the BBC news is divided into 'summaries' and 'bulletins'.

The summaries desk deals with the short news broadcasts which are put out, for example, on the easy-listening channel Radio 2 on the hour and on the half-hour, while the bulletins desk will be putting together the longer, more in-depth news programmes for Radio 4. Both desks will be manned 24 hours a day by a duty news editor and it is he or she who will make the initial decision on the story or stories brought to the desk by the copy taster. Say it's a domestic story which has caught the copy taster's eye, involving a large bank robbery in Liverpool. Having decided to go with the story on a national level – because a large amount of money is involved, perhaps, or many people have been injured, or maybe the bank is even under siege – the news editor has to decide how to deal with it. The news editor has the option of going straight to the BBC's local radio service in Liverpool to get a voice report from a correspondent working at that station; the news editor might, on the other hand, regard the story as sufficiently important to send one of the London-based correspondents to Liverpool to file reports direct from the scene; or a regional correspondent in the area might independently file a report which is sufficient for the news editor's needs. There is no rule as to which source the news editor will go to for the report; it all depends on the circumstances. To make the right decision fast is most important, and that is a skill a news editor picks up on the job; the news editor who consistently makes the wrong decision here will not last.

THE WRITER-PRODUCER

The news editor will then hand the story to the news writer – sometimes known as a news producer. This person's job is to write the story as it will be read on the air. If there is a recorded report to go with the written news piece, the writer-producer will be given this too. He or she will then edit the pre-recorded report (see below) and write the story, or cue, according to a pre-agreed timing. The written text and the edited tape (or disc reference – see below) will then be handed back to the news editor or assistant for checking.

Although the story plus the recorded report will be written and edited to run to a particular length, there is flexibility in the written part. If a late story comes in, requiring the rest of the news bulletin to be shortened to make room, the written section of a given news story – to be read out by the newsreader – can be shortened, either by the newsreader if time is really tight, or by the news editor or the news editor's assistant.

There is also always the chance that a beautifully written story complete with its edited report might be shunted back to a later news bulletin if the late story just in is particularly strong – and long. There is also the possibility that a story can be ditched altogether. This is usually a decision that will be made by the news editor when he or she, along with the assistant editor, is putting the final bulletin together. Needless to say, writers and particularly reporters can often feel rather disappointed when their story is dropped, whatever the reason.

EDITING

There are two types of editing in radio, and both are done almost simultaneously in the case of radio news. There's content editing – in other words, deciding which story is in, which story is out and where each story goes in the running order; and there's tape editing. The former is done by the news editor and assistant editor; the latter by the writer-producers and sometimes the reporters.

Tape editing involves taking a recorded report – which might feature on-site interviews and background sound – and cutting it down so that only the most relevant words and sounds are heard by the listener. This is a skilled job, and often has to be done in a great hurry. In studios where tape is still used this job will be done by listening to the tape, marking the relevant 'edit points' with a special pencil known as a 'chinagraph' and literally cutting the tape with a razorblade and rejoining it.

Most newsrooms today, however, are digital – which means that the final edited versions of news reports will be edited and stored on a hard disk. So, the reports will come in from the reporters – on tape, on disk, by phone or down a line from another studio – and downloaded onto the hard disk. Each report will be given its identification code, which will be called up when the time comes to edit it. The person who is editing the report will 'fast-forward' or 're-wind' it just as he or she might have done with magnetic tape (except there will be no tape going backwards and forwards), but the cuts will be made digitally using a screen and a keyboard. The final edited report will be given not in the form of a short piece of tape on a spool but in the form of a password with which the editor can access the report from the hard disk. There are many different types of digital editing technology, so the above description is non-specific, giving a general idea of how it is done in most studios.

NEWS GATHERING

At the BBC there is a department called News Gathering which is headed by the home news organiser and the foreign news organiser. Their responsibility is to 'look after' the correspondents at home and abroad respectively. They need to know exactly what all the BBC's five services – Radios 1 to 5 – might want from these correspondents, and it is their responsibility to see that the correspondents are able to fulfil these needs.

In some ways the news gathering department acts as the correspondents' nanny, checking that they are well and safe, and able to deliver the reports that are needed from them. The BBC now runs a 24-hour news service, and so its correspondents are often required to be on call for 24 hours a day. For this reason the news organisers need to know where they are at all times of the day and night and how they can be contacted.

NEWS TRAFFIC

Traffic is the part of the news gathering department which co-ordinates the tapes and reports which come in from the correspondents and which sends messages from the station out to the correspondents. When a report comes in down the line from a correspondent, traffic will alert all the relevant departments, via a public address system, that the story is on its way. Anyone who might be interested will listen to it on an earpiece. If there's anything there they want, they know that it has been downloaded on to a hard disk and will be able to retrieve the section which is of interest to them.

INDEPENDENT NEWS SERVICES

There is no radio news service as well staffed and as well resourced in the UK as that of the BBC. That said, there are other news organisations which provide effective news coverage for the many stations across the UK which cannot staff their own news operations.

IRN – independent radio news – is one such organisation (see appendix B). Based in London, the company will run news desks similar to those of the BBC, manned by news editors and assistant editors and through which reports will be checked, edited and approved. Writers will script stories to go with reports and to be read by newsreaders; digital editing will happen as described above and bulletins will be put together which on occasion might be indistinguishable from those broadcast by the BBC. In fact, because IRN operates at much lower staffing levels than the BBC, on occasion it will beat the BBC to a breaking story simply because there are fewer layers through which the story goes before being approved for broadcast.

The principal difference between an organisation like IRN and the BBC, however, is the network of local radio stations, domestic correspondents and foreign correspondents. These resources are also what separates BBC Radio news from pretty well any other radio news service in the world and therefore it is something many in the UK wish to protect.

7

TELEVISION: FROM ITS BEGINNINGS TO THE PRESENT DAY

All too often you will read and hear fierce criticisms of television – all aspects of television, from the level of the licence fee to the quality of the programmes. You will be familiar with criticisms of certain television personalities. And you will be familiar with the complaint that 'they' show too many repeats, or too much sport, or not enough sport, or that there is too much sex, violence and politics on television – or that there is not enough of all these.

Yet, in spite this, it is fairly safe to say that in the developed world watching television is the single most important leisure pastime of the twentieth century. We have a love-hate relationship with the box in the corner of the room. Viewers criticise it; governments try to censor it; politicians of all parties claim it's biased against them; we complain when companies use it to adver-tise – to sway our minds one way or another – yet we respond to those advertisements in droves!

All this proves its power.

WHO STARTED IT?

Whatever it is we don't like about it, we still carry on using it, paying for it, and allowing it to play a significant role in our lives. And for all this we could blame the Scottish electrical engineer John Logie Baird – born in 1888, died in 1946 – who in 1922 began research into the possibilities of transmitting visual images via radio waves and who, three years later, gave the first demon-stration of a television image. After much badgering of a reluctant BBC, Baird's 30-line, mechanically scanned system was adopted by the Corporation in 1929, and in 1936 was superseded by his updated 240-line system. The Corporation switched again, the following year, to a 405-line system developed by the rival Marconi company.

This book won't go into how Baird discovered and subsequently developed the concept of television; neither will it get into the technicalities of one system against the other, or the dispute over whether or not it really was Baird who was first past the post with television technology. A number of scientists were experimenting with television at around the same time as Baird, notably Russian-American Vladimir Zworykin (1889–1982), who is credited by many as being more important to the development of television technology than Baird. It it important to note, though, that it was less than 80 years ago when scientists were merely toying with the idea of sending images over the air. Could any one of them possibly have predicted the multichannel universe in which we now live?

THE BIRTH OF NATIONAL TELEVISION

The world's first regular, national high-definition television service was inaugurated from the Alexandra Palace in north London – then the home of the BBC – on November 2, 1936.

The outbreak of the Second World War saw the suspension of the BBC's television service, and resources were switched to radio. The last pre-war television programme to be broadcast was a Mickey Mouse cartoon, which went on air at midday, September 1, 1939 – television's 'shut-down day'. A full television service was not reinstated until June 7, 1946. As all the history books confirm, however, television didn't really take off as a mass medium in the UK until the landmark year of 1953.

What was significant about the year 1953, as far as television was concerned, was the coronation of Queen Elizabeth II. The first ever full-scale outside broadcast operation was mounted for the occasion and the prospect of pictures of a once-in-a-lifetime event coming live into the family home prompted as many British people as could afford it to go out and buy their first television set. From then onwards television in the UK became a mass medium, although still it would have been impossible to predict what it would become today.

From its beginnings in 1936 and for the next 16 years, the BBC's television output continued very much along Reithian lines (see chapter 2). It fast gained a reputation for technical and editorial excellence, not least when compared with its commercial counterpart in the US, and the ethos behind all of its editorial output remained that of public service. Yes, it should entertain, but the words 'educate' and 'inform' were equally important.

Until the words 'competition' and 'monopoly' reared their ugly heads.

THE COMING OF INDEPENDENT TELEVISION

The fall of the post-war Labour government in 1951 was the catalyst which eventually led to the breaking of the BBC's monopoly as the UK's only television broadcaster. Prior to Labour's defeat, the Beveridge Report, overseen by the Liberal peer Lord Beveridge, was published.

Beveridge had been commissioned to look into, and make proposals on, the future of broadcasting in the UK. The report's main proposals included the continuation of the BBC's monopoly and its funding by licence, both very much supported by Labour. But with former prime minister Attlee now back in opposition and Winston Churchill once again premier of a Tory-governed Britain, the opinions of one of the Beveridge Committee's Tory members, the MP Selwyn Lloyd, were heard loud and clear and played a key role in the imminent reshaping of Britain's broadcasting landscape.

The new Tory government set up a broadcasting study group which issued its report in February 1952, three months before its first White Paper on broadcasting. Both suggested that the BBC's monopoly should be broken – a view shared and widely promoted by Selwyn Lloyd – and a period of fierce debate followed, both inside and outside parliament.

Those in favour of the breaking of the monopoly by the introduction of a service 'sponsored' by advertising simply saw this as a way of broadening and varying this still relatively new phenomenon. Those against, on the other hand, saw the BBC as central to the fabric of British society, and thought that any crude, commercialised competitor could be nothing but destructive. During a fiery ten-day debate in the House of Lords, Lord Reith declared that to introduce commercial competition would be to sell British heritage 'down the river'. And the debate wasn't divided purely along party lines; although Labour broadly objected to competition while the Tories broadly favoured it, the debate divided the latter party in particular, its old school fearing a threat to the establishment from commercial television. In spite of his occasional run-ins with the BBC, prime minister Churchill was against commercial television, and asked: 'Why do we need this peep show?'

Two independent bodies were formed to take the argument outside parliament and out to the people – or to be more accurate, out to a somewhat learned elite. In 1953, the National Television Council, chaired by the Liberal Lady Violet Bonham-Carter and organised by Labour MP Christopher Mayhew, was set up to fight the introduction of commercial television; and the Popular Television Association, with its president the Earl of Derby and its membership including actor Rex Harrison, writer Somerset Maugham and historian A. J. P. Taylor, was set up in response, to warn the public of the dangers of monopoly and to put the case that broadcasting should be treated no differently from the press.

THE BIRTH OF ITV

ITV arrived on September 22, 1955, following proposals outlined in the government's Television Bill, published in March of the previous year. The bill presented a clever compromise in that it permitted the setting-up of privately owned commercial television stations, but specified that they would have to adhere to the guidelines established by a new public body, the Independent Television Association (ITA). The ITA would be responsible to parliament, own the transmitters, appoint and supervise the programme companies and control advertising. (The ITA became the Independent Broadcasting Authority (IBA) in 1972, when Independent Local Radio began in the UK. The IBA was abolished in 1990 as part of Margaret Thatcher's breaking up and rebuilding of the independent television industry, and replaced with a less interventionist Independent Television Commission (ITC).)

The BBC had been preparing itself for the launch of ITV almost as though a war was about to break out. It circulated an internal document called 'The Competitor' which was designed to inform senior executives of as many of ITV's programming and scheduling plans as it could lay its hands on. The Corporation pulled a master stroke on the day of the launch of ITV by killing off Grace Archer, one of the leading characters of its popular radio soap opera *The Archers* – which is still running today (see chapter 4). The episode drew 8 million listeners and dominated the newspaper headlines the following day – putting the launch of ITV in the shade – and signalled the start of a ratings battle which still rages to this day.

Ironically it was the down-grading of the country's exemplary broadcasting industry which was the strongest argument against the introduction of independent television, yet it was the BBC which was the first to use its programming as a competitive tool – or even a weapon – rather than as something which is purely there to inform, educate and entertain.

The BBC–ITV duopoly remained for seven years before BBC2 was introduced as the country's third television channel. The coming of ITV had brought regional television, advertisements and a slightly lighter, brighter, more advertiser-friendly form of programming ('quiz shows and westerns' being the blanket, slightly derogatory term often used to describe such programming) to the UK.

In 1955, with the coming of ITV, the Post Office (which was then broadcasting's controlling body) increased the number of broadcast hours permitted by the BBC and ITV from 45 to 51 per week, with evening programmes beginning at 7 p.m. instead of 7.30 p.m. Such developments were clearly positive on both sides, although while more viewing should generally mean more advertising and therefore more revenue for ITV, more revenue could only come the BBC's way at this time if the number of television sets bought – and therefore licences paid for – increased.

By August 1958, with the number of regional ITV stations having increased, ITV could now be seen by 80 per cent of television owners, while the BBC's audience had declined. The development of accurate audience measurement methods were becoming of crucial importance to both ITV and BBC; ITV had continually to show its advertisers that it was providing the audiences, while the BBC simply had to know that it was continuing to provide a public service which was actually wanted and watched by the public.

Yes, the coming of ITV had caused problems; it had shaken the British broadcasting establishment to its roots. Not only was it stealing audiences with 'quiz shows and westerns', but it was stealing trained BBC staff too, winning them over with higher salaries. How could the BBC pay higher salaries unless more licences were purchased, or the licence fee went up?

But the BBC fought back and remains, today, pretty much an equal force with its independent rivals; although now, for the first time ever, the number of British independent terrestrial channels outnumbers those of the BBC. Will the BBC survive Channel 5? On past record, of course it will.

In the 1990s, ITV has experienced constant radical shake-ups. To most viewers these remain behind the scenes, but some of the ramifications have been perceivable on the screen. The 1990 Broadcasting Act, for example, which saw all the ITV franchises auctioned off to the highest bidder, resulted in the London franchise being lost by Thames Television – highly regarded nationally for its strong television dramas and hard-hitting current affairs coverage – to Carlton Communications. It was hard for viewers in London to lose suddenly the familiar Thames Television logo and a number of familiar programmes.

Since the franchise auctions, the government has altered the guidelines which govern the ownership of the media, and the ITV networks are now in the hands of comparatively few companies. At the start of 1996, for example:

- Carlton Communications held the Channel 3 London weekday broadcasting licence (formerly held by Thames Television) and also owned Central Independent Television, the Channel 3 licence for the Midlands, and 20 per cent of GMTV, the national breakfast-time channel 3 licensee, and a 20 per cent share in ITV news provider Independent Television News (ITN).
- Granada Group owned Granada Television Ltd, holder of the Channel 3 franchise for the north-west of England; it also controlled London Weekend Television, the Channel 3 weekend licensee, and had a six per cent share in Yorkshire-Tyne-Tees Holdings (YTTTV), which owned Yorkshire Television and Tyne-Tees Television. Granada also had a 20 per cent share in both GMTV and ITN.
- The media group MAI had a 60 per cent share in Meridian Broadcasting Ltd, Channel 3 licensee for the south of England, a 14 per cent share of YTTTV, and wholly owned Anglia

Television Ltd, the Channel 3 licensee for the east of England. Anglia owned five per cent of ITN.

- There are a further seven single Channel 3 licensees: Border Television, Channel Television, Grampian Television, HTV Group, Scottish Television, Ulster Television and Westcountry Television.

BBC2, CHANNEL 4 AND CHANNEL 5

BBC2 was launched in 1964, the year the Labour Party replaced the Tories as the party in power and Harold Wilson began his almost unbroken 13-year stay at Number 10 Downing Street.

As with the launch of ITV, the coming on air of BBC2 for the first time – on April 20, 1964 – was marred by something quite outside the Corporation's control: a massive power failure in west London, where the BBC's Television Centre was now situated. The press, needless to say, had fun with this the next morning.

But suddenly the choice of programmes available to the British viewer had increased once again, nine years after the launch of ITV. BBC2 was intended as a place where the BBC could experiment with programmes of a more challenging nature – in terms either of their format or their content. 'Minority' is another word often used to describe BBC2 and its independent counterpart Channel 4 (launched in 1982 – see below), although such a term is more often than not used in a derogatory way by those who see such programming as 'elitist' or 'highbrow' – the sort of channel the BBC thinks we should watch rather than the sort of channel we want to watch. The fact is, however, that BBC2 was simply able to act free from the continuing ratings war in which the now renamed BBC1 and ITV were engaged. And the term 'minority' frequently became wholly inappropriate, as when the hugely popular drama series *The Forsyte Saga* (see chapter 2) drew an audience of 18 million to its final episode.

BBC2 introduced ground-breaking programmes whose formats, if not the programmes themselves, live on to this day. The pre-school series *Playschool*, broadcast on the second day of BBC2, has survived into the 1990s, although in slightly different guises – for example in the form of *Playdays* and *Playbus*. The 13-part documentary series *Civilization*, presented by author and historian Kenneth Clark and two years in the making, has been described as 'a milestone in television history'. The ground-breaking comedy series *Monty Python's Flying Circus* was first introduced on BBC2, as was that other milestone in the history of British television comedy, *Fawlty Towers*.

BBC2 was also the place where Britain experimented with colour. It arrived in 1967, 11 years later than in the US. But even then its introduction was slow; at the beginning, only certain programmes were made in colour (and clearly labelled whenever they were, as if to make those without colour sets envious!); also, it took the viewing public a while to decide whether or not to invest in a colour receiver, particularly those who remembered having to buy a new set in order to receive ITV just 12 years before.

Next came Channel 4, on November 2, 1984. That there had been a gap of 18 years between the launch of BBC2 and the launch of the second independent channel was very much down to the see-saw nature of British politics at that time. One of the tasks of the Annan Committee (set up by the Wilson government in May 1970, and chaired by Labour peer Lord Annan) was to look into the setting up of a fourth channel for the UK. However, the following month the Tories were returned, and Annan's work was put on ice until 1974, when Labour returned to government.

Many of Annan's 174 recommendations made when it finally reported in 1977 (this was, at the time, the most comprehensive report ever made on British broadcasting) were ignored, although the committee had certainly opened up discussions relevant to the future of broadcasting. Among recommendations which were taken up, if not always followed to the letter, were: the setting up of the Broadcasting Complaints Committee, the establishment of the Broadcasters' Audience Research Board (BARB), a joint BBC/ITV audience research system, and the creation of Britain's fourth channel.

The IBA was authorised to establish the fourth channel by the 1980 Broadcasting Act, passed by the new Tory government led by Margaret Thatcher, which had come to power the previous year. Channel 4 was launched on November 2, 1982, to most of the UK but not to Wales – which later won its own Welsh-language channel S4C.

Channel 4 was immediately typified by its enthusiastic embracing of its remit from the IBA, which was essentially that it should cater to minorities, and encourage innovation. Needless to say its attempts at doing so occasionally caused controversy, and the tabloids lapped it up. 'Channel Swore' and 'Channel Bore' were among the nicknames given to the channel by the tabloid press – which waged war on its tendency occasionally to show more sexually explicit material than the other three; to give voice to gay people and other minority groups; and to examine controversial subject matter often regarded as too risky by the established channels.

But the channel has gone from strength to strength, its long-term achievements including the expansion of the British independent production sector – as a publisher-broadcaster the channel produces very little of its own programming; and its role in the revival of the British film industry, as co-producer of the films featured in its prestigious Film on Four series.

We only had to wait another 14 years for the fifth channel. It was decided back in 1987, by a group of consultants acting on behalf of the Department of Trade and Industry, that the UK could sustain a fifth television channel and that the only reasons one hadn't been established up to this point were political – rather than technical or financial.

In November of the following year a White Paper entitled *Broadcasting in the 90s: Competition, Choice and Quality* reported that government studies had established that an additional terrestrial television channel was technically possible, that the new Channel 5 licence should be national, that the output should be required to include high-quality news and current affairs programmes, that the channel should be a 'diverse programme service' and that the ITC should decide how the licence would be allocated.

But it wasn't that easy. In 1990 the ITC invited 'expressions of interest' in the running of a fifth channel, and the following year published a 'draft invitation' for applications for the licence, asking only at this stage for comments from prospective licence holders. In 1992 it invited actual applications for the licence and received one – from a company called Channel 5 Holdings Ltd. It then extended the deadline for applications twice, before announcing it was not awarding the licence.

In 1993 a technical review was announced, with the aim of finding alternative frequencies which might improve reception on existing aerials and reduce the number of VCRs which would need retuning. One of the problems with Channel 5 was that it would require a number of domestic VCRs to be retuned in order to be able to receive the channel (the technical reasons for which we won't go into), and the ITC had decided from the outset that the cost of this would have to be borne by the franchise holder.

After much further debate and sounding of potential licence holders the invitation to apply for the Channel 5 licence was issued once again on November 1, 1994. Just under one year later, on October 27, 1995, the Channel 5 licence was awarded to Channel 5 Broadcasting Ltd, which had offered £22,002,000 for the privilege of holding the licence. The terms of the licence would fill this book; to the viewer and the licence holder, however, probably the most important of these terms was that the channel should be up-and-running by January 1, 1997.

STAR WARS

While most of us tend to think of satellite television as very much a 1980s phenomenon, it first impacted on the lives of British television viewers when in June 1967 the BBC screened *Our World*, the first worldwide television programme bringing together live pictures from around the world by satellite. Many countries offered a live performance symbolising some aspect of its culture or place in the world. The British contribution, a joyfully eccentric performance by the Beatles of their new single 'All You Need is Love', said a lot about Britain at that time.

The developments which were to lead to the establishment of what we now know as British Sky Broadcasting, or BSkyB, began much later – with the publication by the Thatcher government of the document *Direct Broadcasting by Satellite* (*DBS*). The DBS document described what was now possible using satellites and set out the options for how the country could move forward with the technology.

The year 1986 was initially envisaged as the start date for some form of satellite service for the UK following an international conference in Geneva during which satellite positions and frequencies were drawn up for most countries in the world. The now familiar debates raged around the UK, however, with the defenders of our great broadcasting heritage saying that satellite television would simply mean wall-to-wall soap operas and a general lowering of standards all round (and were they right?); while the government of the day struggled to reconcile its free-enterprise ethic with its desire to control the broadcasting industry.

In 1987 the BBC joined with a number of ITV companies which were planning to launch a European satellite service called Superchannel. The financial climate was not right, however, and suffering difficulties Superchannel sold out to a US company before the year was out.

The British government, meanwhile, had at last authorised the IBA to put DBS out to tender. In the spring of 1990 a monopoly licence was issued to a company called British Satellite Broadcasting or BSB. In November of that year Rupert Murdoch, at this time best known as a tabloid newspaper proprietor, launched the rival Sky Television. BSB ran into serious technical difficulties, which led to financial problems, which fast led to the merger between the two rivals – without the IBA's consent. BSkyB was born, but suffered huge losses for some time while running six channels on a fraction of the money the BBC or ITV would spend on just one.

To the amazement of many, BSkyB rode out the storm and announced break-even in 1995. It is now well in profit, and continues to play the role of the bad boy of British broadcasting, charging well over the licence fee for subscriptions and extra on top of that for certain premium channels – and in the case of big events such as the 1996 fight between Frank Bruno and Mike Tyson, extra on top for pay-per-view programmes (see chapter 25).

CABLE

Like satellite, cable television is a delivery system rather than an editorial concept. In other words, it's just another way of getting programmes into the home, and until the mid-1990s, cable had no significant extra services to offer to make people think of it in any other way.

By 1996, around half of the UK was cabled for television transmission; in other words, various cable companies had laid cables to at least half the homes in Britain. Those who then wished to subscribe would only need an extra feed from the street to the living room, where it would be connected to a set-top box.

Most cable services in the UK carry BSkyB's channels, along

with a number of channels brought-in from abroad – such as Discovery and CNN from the US – and a handful of dedicated cable-only channels, for example Live! TV, the service owned and run by Mirror Group Newspapers.

Most cable feeds also offer telephone services (usually cheaper than those offered by the national near-monopoly British Telecom) and a wide range of radio channels.

WHAT IT ALL MEANS FOR JOBS

And it doesn't stop here. Satellite, cable and Channel 5 are with us, but there's a lot more to come. There's digital television; interactive services which will allow both interaction with programmes and the opportunity for viewers to choose what they watch and when – a system known as time-shift television. And then there's the much-vaunted convergence between television and computers, which could see programming appear on the Internet once the new-age of super-powered modems is with us.

But it's important to take stock and consider what this all means as far as jobs are concerned. It was in the early-to-mid 1990s when the full implications of the deregulation which allowed the birth of Channels Four, Five and cable and satellite television were felt. And if we focus on just one area of the British broadcasting industry during that time, the BBC, we see a sorry picture emerge as far as job prospects are concerned as from 1991 to 1995 some 6,000 BBC employees were made redundant.

The rapid growth in television output in the UK in recent years has led to a certain number of new jobs – but as much of that growth has been on the delivery side, most of the new jobs have been in technical and administrative areas. Nothing wrong with those jobs; every job in broadcasting is important. What worries some, however, is that while there are more channels and more companies running them, the programme-making side of the industry is not expanding proportionately. And this is where Britain, certainly, has always shown itself as a world leader. And when people express an interest in working in the British broadcasting industry, the appeal is very often the idea of being a part of an industry whose product is revered the world over.

Fortunately, whatever changes might have occurred and are still to occur in this industry, British broadcasting is still widely respected the world over. In the next few chapters we will look at the structures of the companies which make and broadcast the television programmes we watch day in, day out, the people who make them and their roles in those programmes.

8

TELEVISION: THE PEOPLE

MAKING IT TO THE SCREEN

To the average viewer, a television company or broadcaster is little more than the programmes that appear on the screen. The viewer will watch a set of programmes from a particular broadcasting company and judge it accordingly. For most viewers the sight of a busy newsroom in the background of a news bulletin is as much as they will ever see of a television operation. The odd live talk show or special event – such as a telethon – might occasionally offer more of a glimpse of what goes on behind the scenes, but generally, what the viewer is presented with is a series of cleanly edited, neatly packaged, finished programmes, few of which would ever give the first clue about the work that goes on in order to get that programme produced, paid for and put on the air.

BBC1: HOW IT WORKS

To paint a simple picture of how a terrestrial television station works, we'll take BBC Network Television – which includes the channels BBC1 and BBC2 – as an example. The means to the end in such an organisation – the end being to produce, commission, acquire and broadcast television programmes – involves a surprisingly large number of people involved in a diverse range of jobs.

PROGRAMME PLANNING

First there's the group of people who make the broad policy decisions as to what sort of programmes are going to be shown through the year; where in the day and in the week they will go; whether they will be one-off programmes, series, live or pre-recorded; whether they will be made 'in-house' or by outside contractors (usually referred to as independent producers or plain 'independents' – see chapter 23); and how much money will be allocated to the various programme departments, which will in turn allocated money to individual programmes.

The broadest policy decisions will be made by or in collaboration with the channel's controller – BBC1 and BBC2 each have their own controller – and this person is answerable only to the managing director, and above the managing director, the director-general and the chairman.

The controller will, under the guidance of the financial controller, work with the heads of the various programme departments, along with the head of the planning department, to determine programming policy. The programme departments are each broadly responsible for a particular genre of programming; so there will be a drama department, a children's department, an entertainment department, a factual programmes department, a sports and events department, a music and arts department and so on, some of which will be subdivided. For example, within music and arts at the BBC there is a separate music department; and within the drama department there is a person responsible for serials, another for series, another for one-off specials, another for films and another for programmes produced outside by independents.

All the above, then, will be the people who together decide what goes on to our screens. And basically the lower down the scale we go, the more the person or department becomes restricted in the decisions they can make. So, the managing director will have a very broad input into the programme making and scheduling decisions; the controllers will instigate more specific policy which, when it reaches the heads of the programme departments, will become further restricted by budget (allocated by the financial controller) and the policy decision which has determined how much of a particular type of programme will be shown through a given year.

To take the year 1994/5 as an example, a total of 1,478 hours of sports programmes appeared on the two channels together, as compared with 661 hours of children's programmes, 463 hours of drama and 74 hours of music. This does not necessarily mean, however, that the sports department was allocated more money than the others. Drama programmes are generally expensive and time-consuming to make, while sports programmes are much quicker and therefore often cheaper to put together.

It is BBC policy – dictated by government to both BBC and ITV – to 'contract out' at least 25 per cent of all programme production. So another important management position which ranks alongside those of the programme heads is that of commissioning executive. There are several working across the programme management structure of the BBC, and they work with the various programme heads and supervise all work which is produced for the BBC by independents.

There is also a proportion of acquired programming – that which has already been made, and often for foreign markets (see chapter 24). Big American drama series are the most visible of all acquired programming, but there is other acquired programming across all genres and this has to be found, paid for, and occasionally repackaged and allocated across the schedules. This is coordinated by the head of programme acquisition, who will formulate and carry out BBC policy as regards visiting programme screenings around the world (see chapter 24) and striking deals with producers and broadcasters abroad.

What has been described so far is a management structure. Next we get closer to what actually appears on screen.

FROM PLANNING TO PRODUCTION

Each of the programme planning departments will, at the start of a given period of time, be given a budget, a number of programme hours to fill and a series of deadlines by which the programmes must be ready for transmission. The huge job of coordinating all this to the point at which programme production, acquisition and commissioning is underway, on time and on budget is the broad responsibility of the programme department head, but will involve a vast battalion of staff, each of whom will have a very specific task to fulfil.

An in-house drama production, for example, will first have to be written. This script will have to be commissioned by the drama department either from an outside writer or one working regularly with the BBC (there are few full-time staff writers). The script will then have to be approved, redrafted and edited, and then the production team really starts to expand.

The play – or episode of a drama series – then has to be planned into the running of the department as a whole. It must be given money, resources, time and space. It will need actors, it will need to be designed, dressed, made-up and lit, and it will need music. If there are location shots, these will have to be found and access to them assured. If there are any shots which might disrupt a particular community, then the action must be cleared with police and other locally affected people.

All the people who are assigned to carry out these tasks work under a producer, whose job is to ensure the thing gets made and who thus needs to oversee work and make decisions – particularly of a financial nature – every step of the way. The drama will need a director, who will usually be appointed by the producer (but in collaboration with writer and executive producer or programme department head). The director is responsible for the artistic side of the work, while the producer's role is broadly managerial.

So the work is written, staged, designed, cast, rehearsed, realised, and then performed, filmed, edited, approved; it goes through post-production and then is finally given a broadcast slot. And it is only when that broadcast slot arrives and the viewer turns on the television set that he or she generally knows anything about it, unless the programme has been well promoted beforehand. And the only real information he or she will ever receive about the production process will be from the list of credits at the end which lists pretty well everyone involved (but even then not absolutely everyone – you never see the credit 'Accountant – John Smith', do you?).

And that's just one programme. And even after that has been screened there will still be people involved after the event, paying artists' and other fees, ensuring that the work has been properly stored in the archives, possibly even remarketing the work for foreign markets or video or even a book.

Other programmes in other genres will require different treatment – some may happen live on air in a studio situation; others will be filmed live outside at a sports location or some other event. But all will require large numbers of people to see that all gets done properly and on time. So where do they come from?

THE PEOPLE: THE JOBS

We've already discussed the managers, whose jobs are fairly constant and who can be as 'hands-off' as they wish to be as far as the programme production process is concerned. The managers in an organisation like BBC Network Television are there as much as anything simply to keep such a vast organisation together. For as has been described above, just one single television programme requires many people just to get it made. Then it has to be transmitted, paid for, marketed, etc., etc. Do all the people who do these jobs work at BBC Network Television . . . all the time?

Well, the answer is generally yes. Sort of. The BBC has in-house producers, directors, production assistants, sound engineers, make-up people, wardrobe people, designers, set builders, floor managers, accountants, personnel managers, caterers, cleaners – and many other in-house staff I haven't named by profession. All the above, and more, are required for pretty well every minute of television that is produced by the BBC (and any other company for that matter), and when the production concerned is purely a BBC production the company will usually contract its own staff to do the work.

But it's no longer that simple. As has already been mentioned, no broadcaster, not even the BBC, makes all its programmes itself. The 1990 Broadcasting Act says that 25 per cent of the BBC's network programmes must be produced by independents. That does not mean 25 per cent of all programming; news, continuity and Open University programmes are excluded from that total.

What this means is that the programmes which make up that 25 per cent are made by outside production companies, most of which operate in a very different way from an organisation like the BBC. These companies will not have very many permanent staff; they wouldn't be able to afford them. What they will do is have a small core of full-time employees – a producer or two who would probably be the owners or part-owners of the company; secretaries; marketing staff; and perhaps a few full-time production people who might be called researchers or production assistants. All of the above would be working on pretty-well every production the company was involved in, but many more would also be brought in from outside, on a freelance basis.

FREELANCERS

There have always been freelancers in the broadcasting industry, but never so many as there are today. In the late-1980s, early-1990s reshaping of the industry, many people were made redundant from various positions in both radio and television only to be re-employed in the same or similar jobs as freelancers.

Why? Well, because freelance people don't get paid holidays; freelance people pay their own taxes; freelance people can be taken up and dropped whenever it suits the employer; and (most) freelance people will work all days, all weathers, and through most illnesses – because they need to, because they never know when or from where the next job is coming.

Today, the UK is awash with freelance directors, designers, producers, scriptwriters, sound technicians, researchers, journalists, camera operators – and of course actors and presenters. Some are taken up now and again by the BBC, the ITV companies or a satellite operation like BSkyB, but many also rely on work from the independents, which in turn rely on commissions from the aforementioned companies.

INDEPENDENT PRODUCTION

So the system works like this. The BBC will decide to include a one-off documentary special in its 25 per cent quota of independently produced programming. It may have a company in mind for the production; it may have received a proposal for such a programme and decide to go with the proposing production company; or it might put the production 'out to tender', inviting production companies to come up with ideas and budgets, and then choose the best.

The company which wins the commission will then work out the sort of team it needs according to budget and type of programme, and then the freelancers will be employed – usually for the duration of the production only. How do these production companies find the right freelancers? Word-of-mouth is most important here. If the production company wants a particular director for the project – one whose work it favours or one whose particular skills suit the production in hand – then that director will be approached. If chosen, that director is likely to want to bring in his or her favoured camera operators, who, in turn, might have a sound crew with which they particularly like to work. The director might also have his or her favourite editor – after all, often it is the editor's final touches which make the director's work look so good. No director with any sense will ignore this fact.

So, there evolves a chain of people, all of whom become reliant on each other not just for the work in hand, but for future work too. If a producer or a director has liked your work and also finds you personable, then it's likely you'll be wanted again. More on the bizarre life of a freelancer in chapter 21.

THERE'S MORE THAN JUST THE BBC!

The BBC was our example for this chapter. But there are, of course, other television companies employing people throughout the UK. ITV is different from the BBC in that it is broken up into different companies (see chapter 7). These all operate like mini-BBCs for their own particular region of the UK, broadcasting networked programmes (those which go out on ITV to the whole country) and local programmes, which are seen only locally.

The networked programmes are commissioned by the Network Centre, a central body which decides what programmes are networked and who makes them; and the regional programmes will be made by the respective ITV regional companies or contracted out to independents.

The regional companies will therefore offer permanent employment in most areas. Each ITV company's structure will be different from that of the BBC, although broadly they all have a management structure which at the top decides general programme policy and further down gets into the detail of programme making and commissioning.

The BBC is by far the largest employer of broadcasting personnel in the UK, followed by ITV, BSkyB and then the cable companies. BSkyB makes some of its own programmes – mainly news and magazine-style productions – but most are bought-in. So a company like BSkyB will have mostly jobs in marketing and management and on the technical side of transmission by satellite to offer, while so-called 'creative' posts will be few. What creative posts there are, however, will often require less formal training than, say, the BBC will ask for; will often involve 'multiskilling':

in other words, as a permanent employee you might be required to do more than one type of job; and progress, from general studio dogsbody, for example, to production assistant, floor manager or even director, can be a lot faster in such a company.

And like satellite television, cable is more a deliverer of programmes than a maker of programmes, so again, work in cable television – in the UK in the immediate future at least – will be more related to management, marketing, finance and the technical side of transmission by cable than to programme making.

SUMMARY

This chapter has painted a broad picture of the structure of a television broacasting and production company, using the unique example of BBC Network Television as a model. Subsequent chapters will give more information about how the various companies are structured and what job opportunities they offer – but will do so by looking at the actual jobs themselves. And in the following chapter we start at the top of the production team, with the producer.

9

TELEVISION: THE PRODUCER

WHAT IS A PRODUCER?

The producer is the boss. The producer picks the team, controls the budget, sees to it that the production comes in on time, and in general, makes all the key decisions relating to the progress of a production and the people working on it. Today, the credits of every television programme will name a producer, usually in bold lettering right at the end. But it wasn't always like that.

In the early days of television not all programmes had their own allocated producer. When the BBC was a comparatively small operation with just one channel, which broadcast only about six hours' programming a day, a producer was rarely necessary on most programmes. Back then the department head (see previous chapter) would play the role of producer, deciding and allocating the budget and managing the production from start to finish. It was only really with the coming of independent television and the growth in the industry which accompanied this new competition that the department heads could no longer fulfil this role, prefering to allocate a producer to each production or series of productions and allowing the department head to step back and oversee output in a less hands-on manner.

And as television output became greater and more varied, so different types of producer evolved. For clearly a news producer does a rather different job – and will often come from a different background – from that of a drama producer; and similarly a documentary producer will have a whole different set of responsibilities from those of a comedy producer. So if television producer is your chosen goal in the business of broadcasting, it is worth bearing this point in mind: the successful applicant for a producer's job on a documentary series will very often be someone who knows documentary well. If you've been a researcher on documentaries, if you've been a production assistant on documentaries, if you've done editing on documentaries, or if you've been a director on documentaries you stand a better chance of getting a job as producer of documentary programmes than somebody who hasn't had this experience. But we're jumping ahead here. Before considering how you might eventually become a producer, let's first look at how a producer's responsibilities vary across a number of programme genres.

THE DRAMA PRODUCER

A drama producer employed by, say, the BBC is likely to be given the responsibility for a certain number of hours of programming over a given year. He or she might be responsible for two or three one-off, hour-long specials, or possibly a six-part series of one-hour programmes or a 13-part series of half-hour programmes. So at any given time he or she might be securing the budget for one project; working with the scriptwriter and script editor on another; casting a third and putting pressure on a director to finish a fourth before he or she over-spends. For the purpose of this description let's simplify our drama producer's responsibilities to one single one-off, new television play.

If our producer is being employed by the BBC or one of the major ITV companies, he or she will have been given a budget and an idea of what sort of play is wanted at the end. Had it not been a new play that was required – say the task had been to produce a version of *Othello* – then early attention would have been on what sort of adaptation was required and the next key person the producer needed to find would have been the right director for this type of job. For a new play, however, the first requirement is somebody to write it!

The producer might work with a script editor (see chapter 19) to find the right writer with the right play. The producer or script editor may well know a number of playwrights whose work they favour (the old word-of-mouth thing that will haunt this book and your career) and will probably contact them first. The budget will determine how many plays they can commission; to commission two for a one-off slot would be unusual; it is more common to commission eight for six one-off slots. But for our purpose, let's say one has been commissioned, the playwright is available, and work can commence.

The writer will need to know something about the budget – whether the budget will allow all or any of the play to be shot on film, for example. (Shooting on film is expensive – you can't reuse old film stock; video tape is cheaper but doesn't look as good; etc.) Whatever the budget allows, the writer will be required to write accordingly. It may not allow any 'location' (outside the studio) shooting at all. A studio-only production can be cheap and easy to plan and execute but could mean real restrictions for the writer.

The script editor will help the writer to bring the work in on time and to construct the play so that the minimum of rewriting will be necessary. Meanwhile, the producer will, in collaboration with the script editor, set about the business of choosing a director – whose job it will be to turn the script into a one-hour drama for television (see next chapter). The producer may have a list of favoured directors, one of whom might fit the bill. Or the department head or controller may have suggestions to make. Or the producer (having got the approval of the aforementioned people) may decide to be brave and seek out a (relative) unknown. The latter is the least likely of the three, which underlines the fact that to become a director – particularly in television drama – is not easy.

Once the choice has been made, the producer will collaborate with the director to ensure that the right approach to the play is taken. These collaborations will carry through to the casting process – which may fall on the director, or possibly a casting director who will be taken on by the producer and/or director to oversee this most crucial of tasks.

Through a series of production meetings the producer will then work out a detailed budget plan which the director will have to stick to. If there are location shots – at home or abroad – this job can become complicated. It can involve train tickets, plane tickets and hotel accommodation; and if the cast is a star-studded one, there will be actors (or their agents) demanding that flights and accommodation are of a nature which befits the stars' status. This is where the negotiation skills of a producer are often tested to the limit.

Throughout the production period the producer will be keeping an eye on how much the director is spending in order that the production doesn't go over budget. This is frequently where tension is greatest between producer and director.

And now, in terms of how the remainder of the production process continues, the director might well be considered as the person in charge, the producer having made his or her mark on the production early on in the proceedings. The producer will play some sort of role to the end – he or she might want to see 'dailies' or 'rushes' (unedited rolls of film or tape showing what's been shot in a given day) to be assured that all is in order, or the director and production assistant (see chapter 11) might be entrusted with this job. The producer might well be even more hands-on than this, wishing to be in on every shoot, making last-minute suggestions for script changes and so on. It is equally likely, though, that the producer will in the main be letting things take their course, and setting to work on the next project.

THE DOCUMENTARY PRODUCER

We turn to the role of the documentary producer, abruptly, in order to stress the contrast between this and the role of the drama producer. For while both the documentary producer and the drama producer might be employed by the same company, be responsible for the same number of hours of programming in the year, and earn roughly the same money, they will usually be involved in quite different work.

It is unlikely, for example, that a documentary will begin with a script. In place of the script will be a solid block of research, carried out by a number of people who might include designated researchers (see chapter 15), the director and even the producer if, for example, the subject of the documentary was one in which the producer was an expert, hence his or her involvement in the first place.

As much research of the subject will have been carried out as possible before shooting takes place, because the more knowledge the production team – and particularly the director – is armed with, the less speculative, and therefore the cheaper, the shooting will be. Therefore the producer will be watching carefully the progress of the research project. If, for example, the producer and production team are from the UK and the documentary subject matter is in a faraway place, the producer will be attempting to keep the number of flights made by researchers to a minimum. The producer will also be looking at the cheapest way of getting a crew to said faraway place; some ready-and-willing camera and sound crews will be well-versed in such productions, will have much of the required equipment – even some transportation – to hand and will know short cuts which will in turn cut costs. It is the producer's job to know or to seek out such crews.

What's also strikingly different about a documentary as compared to a drama is that, in many cases, nobody – not even the director – knows exactly what is to be shot until shooting starts. In the extreme case of a wildlife documentary, crews can be kept waiting hours, days and even weeks before the star of their film decides to co-operate, or even make a first appearance. This, of course, is costly, and a documentary producer will have to build all such likelihoods into both the production schedule and the budget. And, in collaboration with the director, the producer will need to have drawn up an alternative plan which will be put into action if that which the crew had wanted to film could not, in the end, be filmed for whatever reason.

And so emerges a range of skills and experience which the documentary producer must have to hand in order to be successful in this genre. They are in many areas quite different from those of a drama producer, and pretty well any other producer.

OTHER GENRES

Further differences occur in the producer's work as we move from genre to genre. In television news (see chapter 22) the producer is more often referred to as news editor, and as such has a range of responsibilities which are shared by producers in all genres. In news the editor, like other producers, will have responsibility for long-term planning, management of staff and the controlling of budgets. The controlling of budgets brings an entirely new set of skills and experience to bear in the case of the news editor, for in extreme cases – the outbreak of the Gulf War, for example – budgets will go, and must go, through the roof. In such a case much of the editor's time will be spent rushing in and out of urgent meetings at which decisions will be made at the highest level about making more staff, resources and therefore money available to keep up the coverage. Here again, with just one example, we differentiate between this type of producer and his or her opposite numbers in other departments.

LIGHT ENTERTAINMENT

Like the drama producer, the producer of light entertainment will be spending a lot of time dealing with performers and their agents. In drama there'll be discussions about fees, type of role, amount of on-screen exposure, etc., while in light entertainment there'll be discussions and deals done over where in the show a particular performer will be placed and for how long, how much of a performer's act must be exclusive to that appearance, etc. Where music and musicians are concerned there's the whole area of royalty and performance fees to be considered and in the case of comedy there are particluar questions of taste, libel and language to be considered.

THE COMMON FACTORS: THE QUALITIES ALL PRODUCERS REQUIRE

There are probably more similarities between producers in all genres than there are differences. Whatever the genre, a producer must be a good manager. It is the producer's job, after all, to manage the two most important elements of a production: the people and the money. All producers must also have the ability to plan long-term; to work on more than one production at a time; to balance the creative urges of the director and production team with the business requirements of the television company which employs them or which has commissioned the production from an independent.

Increasingly, as the independent sector grows and more and more producers own and run production companies which are commissioned by broadcasters to produce and deliver finished products, a producer might require the skill to raise money – for particular productions or simply to fund a company. Such a producer might take a percentage of profits in lieu of salary, and must add entrepreneurial flair and sheer guts to his or her list of qualifications.

THE PRODUCER-DIRECTOR

More than ever today you will see the credit 'Produced and directed by...' at the end of a television programme. This is partly the result of the new broadcasting environment in which jobs are less defined by union grade (as the power and size of the broadcasting unions have been reduced) and more by what's required on any given production. It is also the result of the structure of the new and expanding independent sector, where part of the producer's role might be taken by the person who runs/owns the company and who might in the credits be described as an executive producer (in other words, maximum financial control, minimum hands-on creative control). Here the executive producer might make a handful of important decisions at the start of a production and then leave the director to handle the producer's day-to-day work alongside his or her tasks as a director. The executive producer will then keep one eye on the production or productions in hand whilst at the same time getting on with the crucial job of marketing the company in order that future commissions come in as and when they're needed.

GETTING THE JOB

There are a whole range of skills which can be acquired which will help a producer in later life – qualifications in the management of money or of people, for example – but no one such qualification will guarantee you employment as a producer. What will guarantee you employment as a producer will be the sustained demonstration to a wide range of people that you have experience and interest in making programmes for television.

In television you can arrive at the producer's job via the technical route, having been a camera operator or floor manager. It is also quite a natural progression for a director to become a producer; the director has, after all, been in close contact with the producer, observed the producer at work and been the crucial link between producer and production team.

If to be the producer is your goal, you will probably decide upon one of two routes quite early on in your career. You might try and get into the business whatever way you can, starting with any so-called lowly position, showing willing, learning as you go and taking any job that's offered to you. Eventually, if you're any good, you'll get there. Although it may be a long ride.

Alternatively, you might want right from the start to run your own production company (see chapter 23). To this end you don't necessarily need any of the creative skills required by programme makers; instead, you could work through a business studies course, develop your business skills to the point at which you are able to raise start-up capital to form a company and then gather around you the skilled people required to market and make productions for television. This is following the film industry model, where the people who first set up and later ran the production companies approached the industry from a business angle right from the start. And it was their business acumen which enabled them to gather around them the best creative talent in the industry in order to take their business forward.

Another common way to become a producer is, quite frankly, by accident. You might have wanted to be a camera operator, a scriptwriter or director, and simply discovered along the way that you also had the organisational and other skills of a producer. Such producers are often regarded as the best type, from the point of view of the rest of the production team at least, because they've 'been there' and 'done that' and know what it's like to be just another team member. And that's where we go from here – to look at the other production team members, starting with the creative boss: the director.

COURSES

College and university courses in media, television, film and video do, of course, cover the role of the producer (see appendix A). But it is very unlikely that you would walk from such a course and straight into the job of producer. It will be worthwhile studying carefully the list of contacts and courses provided at the end of this book and talking to people who could offer you work which would lead you towards the producer's job as well as to those offering courses which touch upon the producer's job.

10

TELEVISION: THE DIRECTOR

WHAT DOES A DIRECTOR DO?

The director can be the single creative brain behind a programme, devising, writing, and deciding on the final look, pace and style; or the director can be simply a stage manager, telling camera people where to point their cameras and telling the vision mixer where and when to cut, according to a script. It depends on the genre of programme; it also depends on which company is making the programme and for whom.

With most productions, the director is the most important person on the team after the producer. In the case of a drama, one could argue that the director is as important as the producer, if not more so. Because with drama it is the director who interprets the writer's script; it is the director who has to ensure that this interpretation comes out in the actors' performances; it is the director who tells the camera people how best to capture those performances on film or on tape; and it is the director who, in collaboration with the editor, decides how the production will look to the audience.

If we take the opposite extreme – say a live news broadcast or a simple talk show – the director's role is dramatically reduced, at least at the actual time of shooting. For in a simple talk show, for example, all that is actually required of the director 'on the night' is to be able to capture on camera the conversation that is taking place. This will be done from a control room in which the director can see every shot each camera is recording, and hear everything that host and guest are saying. By following the conversation and the gestures of the two subjects, the director will speak to the camera operators (via a microphone in the

71

control room to headsets worn by the camera operators) instructing them who to focus on and from what angle. Once the cameras have achieved the required shot, the director – or the production assistant or PA (see chapter 11), who will be in the control room with the director – will then instruct the operator to hold the shot. The director can then, at the required moment, instruct the vision mixer (see chapter 19) to put that shot to transmission, in other words, put it on the telly. The talk show will be built up of several hundred such shots which, if properly crafted, will give the best-televised representation possible of the conversation which took – or is taking – place.

Certainly, considerable skill is required here from the director – whose instincts are crucial to such a programme. But these skills are shared with, and also to some extent acquired by, the vision mixer and PA, and in a case where a director on such a show went sick at the last minute, it is feasible that one of them could play the role. The producer or floor manager (see chapter 12) could at a pinch step in too.

Should a drama director call in sick for a day, however, it's very likely that the day's shooting would be cancelled – unless it was something that an assistant director could handle. If there was an assistant director, that is.

As a footnote to this point – and to be certain not to denigrate the role of the director on any type of production – it is important to note that in the case of a talk show series the director will be involved not just in the shooting, but in the long-term planning and design. The look, style and feel of the series will have a lot to do with the director and a lot to do with its success.

WHERE THE DIRECTOR'S JOB BEGINS

In most genres of programming the director's job begins with the script. That would be the case in drama, light entertainment, comedy, and even some documentaries. The director's first job would then be to read, digest and interpret the script, and discuss any changes required with the writer, script editor and producer as early on in the production process as possible. In some cases, the director might also be the scriptwriter; this situation is common in film – take the Hollywood cases of Quentin Tarrantino and Woody Allen, and in television, dramatist Mike Leigh, as examples. If the script were for a drama or a comedy, the director would very soon be considering studio sets and/or locations, and cast.

In the case of a documentary or travel programme, where there will be no full script until shooting has taken place, the director's job will begin with a pile of notes compiled by a researcher. With these, the director will begin to come up with ideas about how the subject matter concerned might be filmed, what effects could enhance the subject and therefore what sort of equipment, crew and shooting time might be required. Once shooting is over, the director might well be the person to write – or at least structure – the script, which might be read by an on-screen presenter, or in voice-over. This might be done on location or back home at the editing stage.

In the case of a light entertainment or music programme, the director will, with the producer, begin by considering what acts should be included in the programme or series of programmes; how the programme should look; what the role of the presenter or presenters might be; and which writers might be brought in to script the presenters' 'links' and other elements of the show which don't involve straight performance by a guest act. In light entertainment, much of the above might well be done before the director arrives on the scene. But as the look of such productions is crucial to their success, the director will have to play a role in the design at the earliest possible stage. And where musical and other performances are concerned, the director might well spend time – with the producer and PA, perhaps – visiting theatres and clubs looking for possible acts for the show or shows or inspecting acts which have already been booked.

In all the above cases, there is very much a sense of the director getting a feeling for the programme or series of programmes to be made before doing anything else. The successful director will put that feeling across to the television viewing audience as it watches the final product.

THE DIRECTOR AND THE PRODUCTION TEAM

The relationship between the director and the production team, on any type of production, is a crucial one. In many respects this relationship is more important than that between the production team and the producer, because the director is with most of the team for most of the time while shooting is underway. Often this period can be pressured, with everyone under a lot of stress. If there is not an element of respect and even friendship between team members the experience can be most unpleasant. The producer can keep his or her distance, even playing the role of 'the bad guy' in order to give the team and the director something to team-up against, thus binding them together. The director, on the other hand, needs to be on everybody's case all the time, and therefore needs to be trusted, needs to command respect and, ideally, even be liked (if that's possible) by the rest of the team. And if a director can establish this complex relationship with team members, then the job is half done.

It will often be the director's job to pick the crew – camera and sound people, along with the production assistant. In many cases these will be allocated to the production by the producer or, in the case of a large corporation like the BBC, by the department for which the production is being made. In smaller, more intimate circumstances, however – such as with an independent production company (see chapter 23) – the director will often have more say over who does what. In the case of the editor, in particular, the director will always want to try and work with a favourite for the simple reason that a good editor can often make rather badly shot material really come to life, thus putting the director in a rather better light than might have been the case. Many directors will therefore fight hard to win their choice of editor.

As important to the director is the production assistant or PA (see chapter 11). The PA's job has traditionally gone to women – which is surprising in the sense that most responsible jobs in broadcasting have traditionally gone to men and yet the PA, it can be argued, is a crucial member of the team. Crucial because (he or) she requires all-round knowledge of the production, creatively, technically and financially and will often stand in for the director or producer at important meetings when they must be elsewhere.

We will go further into the role of the PA in chapter 11, and until then suffice it to say that most directors could not function properly without one. The director, for example, can rely on the fact that at the end of the day's shoot the PA will have a complete, timed record of every shot taken. Such records are crucial in the editing process but are also essential in a whole range of situations in which the director might need, for one reason or another, to recap on work done on a particular day or to date on a particular production.

The PA is often the main point of contact for all members of the production team, including producer and director and technical staff. In this role, if the PA is not careful, he or she can end up being personnel adviser, counsellor and general shoulder to cry on. The importance of the PA must never be underestimated – as chapter 11 will make plain, and as all directors know all too well. For this reason, the choice of PA can be the difference between a happy production and an unhappy production for the director.

BECOMING A DIRECTOR

The director must have sound knowledge of all aspects of television programme production, and so could in theory enter the production business in any job and at any level. The director might start in the business as a researcher – one of the easiest positions to get with no previous experience – or as a camera operator, perhaps.

There are two important points to note if you do aim to become a director by climbing the ladder. First, it doesn't matter how junior you are when you start; there are plenty of post-boy-to-director stories that are around to encourage you. And second, once you are 'in', at whatever level, you are going to have to prove yourself at whatever task you are given, every minute of every day. There are so many people who are keen to take on this, one of the most creative and one of the most prestigious jobs in broadcasting, that anyone who shows the slightest sign of lack of interest will soon give way to the next bright, keen young thing who's waiting around the corner.

VIDEO

One quite recent route into directing for television – and even eventually the cinema – has been through music video. With music video crews often much smaller and very much used to overlapping on job responsibilities, the journey up the ladder to the job of director can be much faster than it might be in film or television.

For example, the music video stylist (or art director – the

person who decides upon the 'look' of the video) could be someone straight out of art college who has gained a certain reputation and a number of contacts whilst studying. Coming in to 'style' a video – maybe for a friend who's in a band – will give that person considerable knowledge of the work of a production team. If the job was well done he or she might well be asked back and at least will have something for the portfolio when applying for other jobs. And in the video world, styling – defining the look of the video by choosing sets, costumes, props and sometimes even lighting – will put you in close contact with the director, the artist (the subject of the video) and sometimes the record company or artist's manager – who is effectively the commissioning editor. If you have proved your worth in this role, you will not be laughed out of the building if you suggest that next time you direct. Directing videos is rather different from directing a full half-hour or hour of television, but on the other hand a number of the skills required are learned fast.

Similarly the producer of a music video could conceivably come into the industry with no real experience at all. He or she might simply start with a phone, a fax machine and a desk and the nerve to offer to get a video made for someone – again a friend in a band or a friend who manages a band. The only skills really required here are the ability to find the creative talent and the ability to manage money and time. Such an experience, however, would again bring you close to the director – who, after all, would be working *for* you! And again to suggest, after such an experience, that next time you direct the video would not be outrageous. Suddenly you're a director!

This, of course, sounds easier than it is. The video production business is as overcrowded as the broadcasting business, after all. The above simply illustrates how it is possible to cut corners in some circumstances.

COURSES

There are courses which will train you in a range of skills including those of the director, but few will guarantee you immediate work in broadcast television. Most drama schools, film schools and universities and colleges with media degrees will run courses which include directing, but don't expect to walk out of one of these and straight into the job you wanted. Few people will take you on without some sort of hands-on experience unless you have established quite a reputation whilst still a student.

Courses such as those offered by the National Film and Television School (see appendix A) will usually require people to have had a considerable amount of experience working freelance in the industry. The British Film Institute (BFI) publishes a directory twice a year which lists a number of short courses available in film and video production, and there are many more such courses privately advertised in media journals and national newspapers. But you are advised to have any course investigated before you accept a place. Ideally, always discuss them with former students – and if the colleges have nothing to hide they should be able to help you contact such people – and ask individuals in the industry about them too. If the industry genuinely believes a course to be worthy and valid, then it's probably worth a go.

SELF-HELP

If you want to end up directing, why not start off by directing? Video equipment today is very cheap by comparison with just 10 years ago, and much of the equipment available in the high-street stores offers sufficient technical scope for you to be able to make a passable short film which would demonstrate a number of your skills.

Such pieces of work included in your portfolio when you apply for jobs can only demonstrate your enthusiasm. Don't worry about technical quality when submitting such work to a potential employer or to a college. Professionals and tutors can see past any technical limitations and would be able to see what you might be capable of should the right equipment be available to you.

All potential employees will agree that to see a person's work, whatever the conditions it was made under, can give the best indication of what they might be capable of in the future.

So get going.

11

THE PRODUCTION
ASSISTANT

WHAT IS A PA?

A better question would be 'What *isn't* a PA?' For a PA is involved in pretty well every aspect of a television production. As has been mentioned several times before in this book, the PA is usually a woman. The precise reason is probably historical/social rather than biological. In other words, many might say that women make the best PAs because they're level-headed, logical in thought, cool and non-aggressive under pressure, have organised minds, are more diplomatic, etc., etc. And while all those qualities would help in the job of a PA (they would help any job, in any profession, actually!), it's probably rubbish to say that all women have those qualities, and that that's why all PAs are women. It is more likely that many such roles – in any industry – are taken by women, because the next position up is usually held by a man.

Think of top-level secretaries in almost all walks of life; they're often crucial to the running of massive corporations. And why are such posts so often held by women? Well, imagine if such a job were given to a man, and that the man – as so many women do – soon proved himself thoroughly knowledgeable about all aspects of the organisation concerned, and thus indispensable. What a threat that man would be to the man he was supposed to be assisting! Put a woman in that assistant's role and the 'man-at-the-top' feels less threatened.

And, incidentally, the PA comes fairly low down in the salary scale on a production team. Can you imagine that being the case if this crucial job were typically done by a man?

But we're getting a touch socio-political here. Do you prefer the former explanation? That women are biologically more suited to the job of production assistant? Or the latter, more controversial one? You choose . . .

The PA is essentially the personal assistant to the director and, at times, the producer. Usually the PA is assigned to a programme right from the start and stays with it to the end. PAs will control budgets, do most of the organisation, sit in on meetings with the producer and/or the director, and in the absence of either, will sit in on their behalf.

Often, on a big production, there will be a studio PA and a location PA. As the titles suggest, the location PA will assist the director on all location work, while the studio PA will assist the director in the studio. On location the PA will attend to matters of transport, accommodation and meals, and will be at pains to ensure that everyone – crew and performers – gets to places on time and with the right equipment. Here the likely problems are hard to predict; if a particularly temperamental crew member or performer doesn't like his or her hotel room, it is likely to be the PA who has to sort it out. If it rains when the day has been planned for a shoot in the sunshine, it will be the PA who has to co-ordinate the necessary change of plan and changes in the shooting schedule. On location, the PA will also be responsible for recording, timing and numbering each shoot so that the director and producer have a full and accurate record of what was done on each day.

In the studio, the PA will be responsible for booking the studio time and ensuring that the right equipment is there, and the right-sized crew. The PA will have to reserve dressing rooms for artists, make sure that make-up people know what's required (particularly special requirements for particular performers) and when they're needed, and ensure that everyone has the right script for the role they are playing, either in front of or behind the camera. When scripts are changed at the last minute it will be the PA who notes accurately the changes that are to be made and it will probably be the PA who makes the actual typed changes and then distributes the new version to the relevant people. The PA will also organise the final planning meeting at which all the people required for the studio will be present and discuss last-minute requirements and strategies.

During actual recording or live transmission the PA's job becomes even more crucial, for here he or she becomes the eyes and ears of the director. The PA will alert the camera operators to the next shot on their camera script; will instruct the vision mixer to cut from one camera to the next; will time all the shots; will warn director and producer if the programme is running late; and after the recording will attend the editing session to ensure it goes according to timetable. Timing is crucial in all such situations, as anything that goes over time usually costs extra money. This fact alone puts considerable pressure on the PA at all times.

THE PA'S JOB IN DETAIL

It is worth examining the work done by a PA a little more closely, partly because it gives a clearer picture of quite why this job is so crucial to a production, but also because it sheds some light on the work done by pretty well every other team member.

SETTING UP

At the start there's a lot of paperwork. This will partly be generated by others – producer and director in particular – as they send the PA memos reminding him or her that this or that will be required before production begins. Other paperwork will be generated as the PA begins to book facilities and equipment. The PA will need to keep records of all such bookings – and any purchases too – both for proof that they were made and for budgeting purposes. For yes, it is the PA who controls the budget, too. In fact, think of it this way: the producer decides and allocates the budget, the PA controls the budget and the director spends the budget. Once again, the PA is stuck in the middle.

Then there's the cast, or the presenters, to consider. There may be a casting director on the production (if it is a drama or variety show with a reasonably high budget), in which case the PA will have little to do with choosing or booking actors. In cases where there is no casting director, the PA will often help the director with the checking of artists' availability and the arranging of auditions.

Once artists are selected, detailed contracts must be drawn up and sent to the respective agents, and all or part of this job will once again be down to the PA.

And so more paperwork is generated. All this paperwork must be kept in a production file or files, and these must be guarded carefully by the PA, for they are what becomes the production bible. Anything and everything that has gone on will be in these files and they are likely to be called upon many times during and even after a production. Another weight on the PA's shoulders.

THE FINE DETAILS

Many productions have researchers attached to them – but many others don't, and the finding out of certain facts and figures relating to the production – either in editorial content or in the execution of the production – might fall to the PA. So, if a particular historical fact is required (perhaps by a presenter who wishes to make a passing remark about something; or by the director who wants to know whether keeping a particular building in shot will damage the historical accuracy of a particular drama), then it may well fall to the PA to go and find out the relevant information – from a library, a town hall or a museum, for example.

Other fine details might concern the copyright of a piece of music, a piece of written work (part of a poem or play, maybe) or even a work of art – which the director might wish to feature in a production, for whatever reason. It could well become the PA's responsibility to check the copyright status of the work in question, and if payments are required, to make the necessary arrangements.

Then there's insurance, and other outside regulations governing where a film crew can and cannot shoot. The use of children and animals in programmes can involve particular special arrangements and it will often be down to the PA to know what is and what isn't permitted in such – and other – special cases, and to make provisions accordingly. And all this before any real work has started.

SCHEDULES AND RUNNING ORDERS

There are rehearsal schedules, outside broadcast (OB) schedules and studio schedules; and there are running orders. All these amount to detailed lists which show when something is to happen and how long it should take. They may be worked out by the producer, director, floor manager or PA – or a combination of these – but the final drafting and making sense of these lists are down to the PA.

The rehearsal schedule will usually be a straightforward list detailing who should be rehearsing where, when and with what.

OB schedules will detail considerably more, like: where, when, how to get there, where to park, who's involved and when and where; accommodation details; information about meals and meal times; and availability of other facilities like doctors, shops, telephones, etc. That will be the general schedule. Then there will be day-to-day schedules which will detail location; 'call' times (who's wanted and when); important names, addresses and phone numbers of people involved in that day's shoot; catering; transport; and shooting breakdown including location and names of the technicians and cast involved.

Studio schedules will include details of technical facilities and personnel requirements along with accurate timings of what will happen in which studio involving whom – on an hour-by-hour basis. Along with this broad schedule there will also be recording schedules which detail what page in the script relates to which shot, camera position and so on. The working out of such details is, of course, down to the director, but once again the responsibility for the presentation of these schedules is that of the PA.

In live situations – say, in a news programme – the running order will detail exactly how long everything has to take, what is 'live' and what is pre-recorded, when and where the pre-recorded sequences are fed in and how long they take. In a live situation everyone will be armed with this running order and will stick to it like glue. If it is accurate and correct, then everyone will know what his or her job is, when it has to be done and how it fits in with everybody else's. The PA is most likely to be the person who puts the final running order together, under the instructions of the director and possibly the floor manager and producer. And if it's put together wrongly, guess who's likely to get the blame!

THE SCRIPT

Unless the script arrives in perfect shape (type-written, at least triple-spaced, copy down the right-hand side of the page to allow room for director's notes, camera directions, etc. on the left), then it will be down to the PA to get it properly typed-up – either by instructing someone to do it (a production secretary, for example, if there is one) or by doing it him or herself.

In the case of a studio production, where there are several

cameras, a detailed camera script will also be required. This again might be rather poorly detailed on paper by the director – perhaps in collaboration with the camera operators and the floor manager (see chapters 12 and 13) – but once again it will need to be properly presented and copied for distribution to those who will require a copy on the day. And yes, the job of presenting it properly is likely to fall to the PA. The PA will also want – or be asked – to check it over to make certain that it is technically feasible. Can a camera be at position A for that shot and be ready to be in position B for the next but one shot? And in the course of the repositioning, will cables cross, or a prop or an actor be disturbed? Now you can start to see how all-encompassing skills and knowledge of production are a necessity for the PA.

Scripts will, of course, vary in detail and in nature depending upon the type of programme. In a live political discussion programme, little more than a running order with 'in cues' and 'out cues' can be prepared. And in the case of a discussion programme which gets really vital or heated, what script or running order there was might well have become of little use. If it is effectively 'torn up' because the programme has taken a completely different form from what was intended, then the job of the PA becomes crucial in the sense that timings will have to be reworked, and there will be little time to rewrite them and distribute them to the relevant people. So this will all have to be relayed in 'talkback', in other words, the facility which allows the director and others in the control room to communicate via microphones and headset to everyone on the studio floor.

TIMINGS, COUNTING AND STOPWATCHES

In a live or an as-live programme, the running order – which indicates what item comes when, where from and how long it will take – will be changing right up to the moment of transmission (if the programme is live) or recording (if the programme is as-live). As-live simply means that, as far as possible, the programme will be made as though it is being broadcast live. This is done both to give the feel of a live programme and to enable a programme to made as close to transmission time as possible. A programme made as-live is effectively edited as it goes along, so by the end of the recording time, you virtually have the whole programme ready to go out, timed to the second – by the PA, of course.

In such a programme – say a half-hour live news programme (see chapter 22) – timings on the running order will change every second, right up to the start of transmission. This is because fresh news items will be coming in until the last minute – either written items or items recorded on videotape. To accommodate these, other items will have to be dropped or shortened, and this will constantly mess up the timings. The PA is the person who has to keep the programme to the right length as these new items come in and other items are dropped. It's a job of mental arithmetic right up to the last minute. Is your head clear enough?

When it comes to the time to record – or to transmit direct – the PA really comes into his or her own. Are all the taped inserts there, in the right place, in the right order and properly marked? Does everyone have the right script? Is everyone in the right place? Are the required graphics ready? The checklist is endless.

Then when the programme is up-and-running the PA is juggling an enormous number of skills – with one eye on the running order/script/camera script he or she will be telling the camera people which shot is coming up next and which camera should be on it, ready for the director to instruct the vision mixer exactly when to cut to that particular camera. The PA will also have another eye on at least one stopwatch with which he or she will be making sure that nothing over-runs, and that various inserts, graphics and music come in on time. This stopwatch will have been set at zero at the start of transmission or recording – or maybe will have been set at, say, zero minus 24 minutes (if the programme is to last 24 minutes) so the PA has a clear picture of how much time is left to run. Some PAs will refer to several stopwatches at one time – one may be timing the whole pro- gramme, while another may be there to time each insert, etc. All such variations depend upon the PA, the type of programme and so on.

On location, the job of timing will be different. Suffice it to say that timing, before a production begins, during rehearsal, during recording, filming or transmission and afterwards – at the editing stage, for example – is crucial in television broadcasting, and ultimately it is always down to the PA to see that it is properly done.

POST-PRODUCTION

Post-production refers to the process during which all the raw footage and sound recordings are edited together, in sequence, and any graphics or other effects required are added. It depends on the director, editor and the type of production how much involvement the PA has here, but as the person who has the production bible, full knowledge of every shot taken and its duration, the PA will rarely get out of some involvement in the editing process.

Then there are the more mundane after-production duties to be considered: costumes and other hired equipment to be returned; the 'logging' of any copyright music used to be done so that proper royalties are paid; actors, presenters, contributors and other staff to be paid. There are people to be thanked – sometimes with letters or cards, and other times with presents. A post-production script might have to be prepared which details the final content and timings of the final production as it went out or as it was recorded. This is for the records and will be kept with the recorded version of the programme in the archives.

The channel's presentation people will want information about the programme, stills and even a pre-recorded trailer if it is to get prominent billing in the weeks and days leading up to transmission. It will probably fall to the PA to organise this. And if there is to be publicity for the programme – a launch party or screening for the press, press releases, etc. – then the PA is likely to be involved here too.

It's as though you can never get away . . .

HOW TO GET THE JOB

A college or film-school course which offered useful background for someone aiming at becoming a PA could never properly prepare someone for the job which has just been described. Clearly, in the case of the PA there is no substitute for experience in production.

Many PAs currently working in the industry started out as secretaries in large organisations like the BBC or one of the ITV companies – perhaps to producers, programme controllers or television company department heads. In this position they will have had access to information about company training courses for PAs which they will have attempted to join, or maybe will have been permitted a break during which hands-on production experience could be acquired.

Other PAs will have started out in a small independent production company (see chapter 23), where everyone at least sees what the other members of the team get up to. Even a supposedly 'lowly' job like runner (basically a messenger who takes film from the shoot to the processing lab and other such jobs) is a good starting point. And on a small production or in a small production company, a runner with talent and initiative would soon get noticed.

All PAs will tell you that there's no substitute for experience. And given that most people say that a PA requires a particular type of personality – patient, diplomatic, thorough and unflappable – then watching one at work will help the would-be PA to ascertain whether or not he or she fits the bill.

If you want to do the job, then you simply have to prove to as many of the people who count – and two of the most important are the producer and the director – that you can do it. And once you've done it once, successfully, you've probably got pretty well all the work you'll ever need. As a PA, at least. For there are small television production companies, video companies, facilities houses and other organisations which will never permanently employ PAs and will always require freelancers (see chapter 21). Make a name for yourself as a good, hard-working freelance PA and you will often find yourself in the enviable position of being able to choose which jobs you'd like to do and to turn down the ones you don't.

12

THE FLOOR MANAGER

WHAT DOES A FLOOR MANAGER DO?

The floor manager is one of the few 'behind the scenes' people you will have occasionally seen on television. For very occasionally, particularly on live television, the presenter will grab the floor manager and engage him or her in a few seconds of supposedly off-the-cuff comic chat. It gives the impression of a relaxed, informal and very live situation – and the floor manager is always the one who's singled out because he or she usually isn't glued to a piece of equipment – like a camera or a 'boom microphone'.

You might also have seen the floor manager on occasion down at the front of a studio audience giving the signal as to when its members should clap, scream, laugh or even moan in disapproval. So will you get famous as a floor manager? Answer, no. You'll work with the famous, though . . .

During a studio recording, the floor manager is the director's representative on earth. The floor manager's job begins usually just a few days before the production moves into the studio, and he or she will receive the first full briefing on the production at the last big planning meeting prior to the start of recording – or transmission if the show is going out live.

· Once recording is underway the floor manager's two main areas of responsibility will be liaison between director and studio staff, and management of what actually happens on the studio floor: hence the title.

ON THE DAY

Before the recording of a programme in a studio – or before the transmission of a live programme from a studio – the director and producer will be frantically involved in last-minute preparations, sometimes in the studio, or maybe outside the studio, in the production office or in the control room or gallery. It is therefore left to the floor manager to organise and be responsible for everything that needs to be done in the studio before the red light goes on.

If there's a studio audience, the floor manager – along with any front-of-house staff who may be involved – will be seeing to it that everyone is seated in good time. Cynically, some might say, the floor manager might also be required to see to it that only the best-looking members of the audience are in the seats which might occasionally get caught on camera. The floor manager will be careful to see that no rows of empty seats will appear on camera and so on.

The floor manager will also be making sure that any sets which have been built are safe, finished and in the right position in relation to the cameras and camera script. He or she will walk any guests through their movements – however few movements they may have – and will instruct musicians and other performers where to stand.

SAFETY

Safety in the studio is crucial, as there is much heavy equipment being swung around at some speed (cameras, camera 'cranes', 'boom' microphones, etc.) as well as high-voltage cables passing across the floor in all directions. Most of the crew will be well versed in safety procedures and will know only to step on cables if they are protected by 'duck boards' (small ramps), to steer clear of a moving camera and so on. Guests – sometimes unin-itiated members of the public – are generally not aware of such hazards however, and where such people are concerned the floor manager has the responsibility to inform them of what's going on in the studio and to keep them away from any danger. The same goes for members of the studio audience.

The floor manager will also be ultimately responsible for ensuring that all props and technical equipment are sound, stable and safe. As a camera is moving rapidly from one side of the studio to another to prepare for its next shot, the floor manager will be watching for cables which might get caught or damaged in the process as well as anyone or anything which might run the risk of being hit by this heavy piece of equipment moving at high speed.

ON AIR!

In the minutes leading up to the start of recording or live transmission, the floor manager might act as an audience warm-up person, cracking jokes to loosen them up, whilst reminding them of the basics like when to clap, when to be silent, when not to look up at the ceiling monitors and so on.

During the recording of a programme, or the transmission of a live broadcast, the director will be up in the gallery or control room, some way away from the studio floor and certainly not in earshot of anyone on the floor. The director will, on the other hand, be in direct radio contact with the floor manager.

During recording or transmission, the director will pass any 'cues' or 'prompts' to guests or presenters, via the floor manager. The floor manager will employ a type of sign language which will be familiar to all presenters and which will warn when time is running out, how long an interview has to run, which camera to look into and so on. Some of these instructions will already have been included on the shooting script or running order; others will come 'live' into his or her headphones from the director.

The floor manager might also communicate with presenters and guests via 'idiot boards'. These are large boards with instructions daubed on them with a large marker pen. They will be used to prompt the presenter on occasion, and also to inform the presenter of any sudden change of plan which might have occurred.

At the end of a recording session the floor manager will play a part in the breaking down of the studio, in other words, seeing that the props department properly and safely dismantles the equipment it is responsible for and that the technical staff do the same. And once the studio is left as it was before the production moved in, the floor manager's job is effectively over.

BECOMING A FLOOR MANAGER

Large organisations like the BBC, the ITV companies and even BSkyB will employ full-time floor managers who will be assigned to in-house jobs on a year-round basis. To get to that position is not easy, but it is possible to rise to floor manager from pretty well any job.

A runner, or anyone on the technical side – lighting, sound or props – could work his or her way up to the floor manager's job and, of course, with all the studio experience the floor manager has, the job can serve as a rung on the ladder to becoming a director.

As with the PA (see previous chapter) there is a certain type of personality which is best suited to the job of floor manager. Someone who panics would not fit the bill; there can be last-minute changes made during a production which the floor manager might have to communicate to a presenter or on-camera guest without the television audience being at all aware that anything out of the ordinary has happened. Accidents can happen in the studio too, and in the first instance it will be down to the floor manager to take charge.

A pressured job, but a rewarding one, particularly in the sense that a floor manager can move around from production to production and gain wide experience of different types of programme in a comparatively short period of time.

13

THE CAMERA OPERATOR

GOODBYE, CAMERAMAN

Camera operator. It just doesn't sound as slick, or as prestigious, as the term 'cameraman', does it? The term 'cameraman' conjures up the idea of the rather macho guy with a lightweight video camera slung over his shoulder as he runs, ducks and dives whilst shooting news footage of urban warfare in the Middle East. Or maybe it brings to mind the Hollywood movie cameraman sitting in regal pose behind a monster piece of equipment which might be on a huge crane, on a fast-moving truck following a cowboy on a horse, or on a vast sound stage, shooting a massive Cecil B. de Mille crowd scene or a complex Busby Berkeley dance sequence. That's a cameraman. A camera operator? Well, that sounds like some sort of technician; just one of a crew.

But in fact they're one and the same. It's simply time to stop calling them cameramen. They were almost all men in the beginning; the equipment was dangerously heavy and it was an all-male world when television began back in the mid-1930s – and even more so when films began back in 1895 or thereabouts. But today a camera need not be the cumbersome, heavyweight lump it used to be; and women are doing many more of the jobs which used to be almost exclusively held by men. So cameraman is out; and camera operator it is.

NEW TECHNOLOGY

Chapter 2 discussed briefly how technological developments have changed the broadcasting industry – the media as a whole – so radically in recent years. Those developments have had their most profound effect on the industry's delivery systems: video; satellite and cable delivery; digital technology; on-line and off-line multi-media. As far as individual jobs are concerned, however, new technology has had more of an effect on some than on others. Nowadays the producer can call up budgets, scripts, cast lists and schedules on a computer so that massive files don't have to be stored and carried around; the PA can write and rewrite running orders on a word processor so that everything doesn't have to be retyped the moment something happens to change the script, cast or schedule; editors can use digital systems, which means that scenes and frames can be accessed instantly and cuts and joins made without the need to wind and rewind videotape constantly; but otherwise many jobs remain pretty much the same. And often, the benefits of new technology are felt by the people using it rather than the television viewer at home.

But the camera operator's job has been radically affected by new technology, to the point that it has changed the nature both of his or her work and of the finished product we see on our screens.

For example, the news. It wasn't so long ago (the late 1970s) that the terms 'ENG' and 'PSC' were introduced. PSC stands for Portable Single Camera; ENG stands for Electronic News Gathering, a term coined when lightweight video cameras seemed almost overnight to replace film crews for shooting actuality for news bulletins. News footage shot on film required quite a large crew: lighting is more crucial where film is concerned; sound is recorded separately and so requires extra equipment and personnel; film reels have to be stored, loaded and replaced with care and therefore require an extra technician. That film then had to be motorbiked to the film processors, processed and then motorbiked on to editor for cutting and synchronisation of sound before it was ready to be inserted into a news bulletin.

News footage shot on video – on a PSC – is quite different, however. Masses of reels of film aren't required because you can reuse tape; videotape records sound and image simultaneously, so it doesn't have to be synchronised at the editing stage and less equipment is required; and most important, videotape doesn't have to be processed, so the whole motor bike-to-processor-and-back-to-editor process disappears.

So, suddenly, with the introduction of ENG, news bulletins looked different, as the images were more up to date. The news bulletins also looked different because the new lightweight video cameras (usually slung over the shoulder of the camera operator and not always requiring any extra personnel) could reach places the cumbersome film cameras couldn't. Suddenly camera operators could find themselves ducking snipers' bullets. ENG brought reality to the news. It also reduced the size of the film crew required to shoot an insert for a news bulletin. The unions did much to resist the introduction of ENG; or at least, they tried for a while to maintain the size of the crews. But meanwhile, new equipment meant that new types of image were coming to our screens – and to an extent these required a new type of camera operator.

WHAT THE CAMERA OPERATOR DOES

So far we have only discussed the news camera operator – whose job can be terrifying and dangerous if he or she is reporting a war, for example; and on occasions dull and boring, for example when he or she is standing outside the Houses of Parliament in the cold and dark waiting for a late debate to end in order to record an interview with a number of key politicians as they leave the building.

So there are varying degrees of excitement and satisfaction in this job, which the uninitiated often consider is the most romantic and thrilling of all the jobs in film and television. And there are varying degrees of excitement and satisfaction whatever the production. It's true that most camera operators offered work on a documentary about fishing in the Caribbean would jump at the chance without asking too many questions. But there are unpleasant moments to be encountered even during such a seemingly ideal job. Hours waiting for the right fish to bite can be tedious however perfect the surroundings; hotels, even on some Caribbean islands, rarely live up to expectations; and temperamental crew members can turn the most idyllic job into total misery.

Suffice it to say, therefore, that if you're not in it for the creative satisfaction – or perhaps ultimately as a means to becoming a director – then the camera operator's job will not necessarily be for you.

In television, the camera operator is the eyes of the director. For it is usually the director who decides what will be shot, and the camera operator who interprets that decision. That rather makes it sound as though anyone could do the job, but that, of course, is not the case. For it's not a question of simply pointing a camera wherever the director tells you to point it; it's more a case of having an understanding of what the director wants, and providing it as quickly and as effectively as possible. A camera operator must understand picture composition, the balance of light and shade, just how close a close-up should be and how far away a long-shot should be. A camera operator can suggest shots, but this can only be done once an understanding and a rapport have been built up with the director. A camera operator must truly understand the production, its style and its audience, and must be able to interpret directions according to that understanding.

On some productions, the camera operator will follow the director's instructions to the letter, little or no rapport will be established, wanted or required, and the camera operator will not in the end have made much of a mark on the end product, other than having allowed the production to have gone ahead in as smooth, and as professional, a manner as possible.

On other productions, the camera operator and director might be good friends, having worked together for years. In such a case the camera operator might suggest a number of changes to the director's plans, and might even suggest entirely new approaches to the production. Such synergy between camera operator and director can result in an excellent finished product; it can also save a lot of time on set or on location, as it will generally take less time for the director to explain things to the camera operator. An ideal situation and, surprisingly perhaps, not that rare.

As well as interpreting the director's ideas, it is also the camera operator's duty to understand the equipment he or she is operating. Many freelance camera operators will own their own equipment and bring it along to the job as part of the deal. In such a case maintenance would be carried out by the camera operator or a colleague who would work alongside him or her at all times. But even in the case of a camera operator who was using hired or in-house equipment, a rudimentary knowledge of how to maintain and, in an emergency, repair equipment would be expected.

And so a picture builds up of the camera operator as a skilled, creative person. But before we look at how these skills are acquired, we will look briefly at the role of the camera operator in different genres of production, and at the members of the camera crew without whom the operator could not function.

FILM OR VIDEO?

Film and video are radically different media, and nowhere does the difference between them show itself more clearly than where the role of the camera operator is concerned. Film is an expensive medium; if you mess up on film it costs time and money. Video is a cheap medium; if you mess up on video it only costs time. For film is a chemically treated material which reacts to light; expose it to light and that reaction cannot be reversed. You can't reuse it. If you've exposed it properly – got what you want on it – fine. If the shot hasn't worked, for whatever reason, you'll have to do it again – with a new piece of film, which will have to be paid for. Video, on the other hand, is a magnetic material which picks up and holds an image for as long as you want it there. If you mess up on video you can rewind it and record on it again and again. And even if you don't want to reuse it, videotape is considerably cheaper – and easier to store and lighter – than film. Also, you don't have to go through the business of processing videotape to see whether or not you got the shot you wanted first go.

So to start with, the video camera operator's job is perhaps easier and certainly less pressured than that of the film camera operator. And when are the different media used? As a general rule, film is used to make feature films (for theatrical release and television), high-budget television dramas and high-budget theatrical and television documentaries; and video is used for news footage, studio-based light entertainment and talk shows, low-budget drama (soap opera and some situation comedy) and low-budget documentary and magazine programmes. The reasons why film and video divide themselves between programme genres in this way are partly historical and partly practical, and we won't go into them here. To explain what the two media mean to the work of a camera operator is more important.

If you're using film you're under more pressure to perform well first go. And if you're using film on a major production, there will be a slightly different team structure around you. For on big-budget film productions – certainly in the cinema – the camera operator will work to the instructions of the lighting camera operator, also known as the cinematographer or director of photography. On a big-budget film the lighting camera operator (LCO) is an important figure, often almost ranking alongside the director. For the LCO will make the big decisions about the filming process: what equipment, what lenses, what camera angles and what type of lighting are required. This will all be done in consultation with the director. On a big production the LCO will rarely operate the cameras. He or she will have done so in the past, however, and this will have given him or her the knowledge with which to pass on ideas and instructions to the camera operators.

In television the equivalent to the LCO is often called the lighting director. He or she will make similar decisions to those made by the LCO on film, but usually on a smaller scale. The lighting director will often have moved up through the ranks of a camera crew (see below), but might also have previously worked as a lighting technician, for example. Possibly even in the theatre.

So a picture develops, not just of a lone camera operator, but of a team all working to the director but who, together, create or record the basic raw materials of any film or television production: the pictures.

THE CAMERA CREW: FILM

Below the camera operator – in a film crew rather than a video crew – is the camera assistant. On a small shoot the camera assistant will carry out pretty well all the tasks relating to the camera and the camera operator's work, but will rarely actually operate the camera. So the camera assistant will look after the maintenance of the equipment; keep the PA informed as to how much film stock has been used and advise if any more will be required; drive the camera and camera operators around if required; organise the moving of equipment through customs and so on if any foreign travel is required; set up the camera and load it with film on location; assist the camera operator with any difficult shots; and operate the clapperboard at the start and sometimes at the end of each take. The camera assistant will also be responsible for safety at all times where camera equipment is concerned.

On a large shoot the camera assistant will work alongside a team of people whose jobs will be quite specific – such as the grip, the loader, the clapper-loader and focus-puller – all those names so many of us see roll up at the end of the film, wondering 'What on earth does that person do?' The grip will be responsible for the physical moving around of the camera – operating dollies (like large moving tripods) and cranes (for high overhead shots), laying tracks (like railway tracks) for tracking shots (following someone down a road, for example) and driving the camera crew and equipment around. The focus-puller will be responsible for ensuring the camera is the right distance from the object being shot for it to be in focus; will occasionally actually adjust the focus of the camera during a shot; and will always be responsible for the care and maintenance of the lenses. The loader, meanwhile, loads and unloads the film; and if the job description extends to clapper-loader, then this person is also responsible for chalking the right information on the clapperboard (or keying it in on the more modern versions which come with their own VDU) and 'marking' the beginning, and sometimes the end, of a shoot by holding it and clapping it in front of the camera. (Many wonder why a single 'clap!' of the clapperboard is made at the start of each shoot. This is because with film, sound and image tracks are recorded separately – sound on magnetic tape; image on film. When these come together in the editing suite the visual 'clap' at the start of the film can be lined up with the audible 'clap' at the start of the audio tape. This way sound and image can be synchronised at the start of each shot.) The loader will also keep records of the type of film stock and equipment used as well as the light readings so that the processing laboratories know exactly how to treat the stock when they receive it at the end of the shoot.

THE CAMERA CREW: VIDEO

In a television studio, where video (or electronic) cameras are almost always used, the camera crew usually comprises only the camera operators and one or a few general camera assistants. In some circumstances grips will be required, but it is rare that as many assistants are used in a television studio, simply because there are other people around who take care of the equivalent work.

For example, the cameras record on to video tape recorders (VTRs) which are situated in the director's gallery or in the control room nearby, so there is no loader required. Clappers aren't required either, because usually each shot will be marked with an electronic identity card or 'ident' which will be organised by the PA. Any camera assistants who are required will mainly be moving cameras around inside the studio – clearing cables out of the way (television cameras are electronic and require a high-voltage power source) and driving the motorised cranes when they are used. With very small studio shoots, where the camera or cameras are required to move very little, such jobs might be carried out by the floor manager. Camera operators in the studio will work very much more to a fixed script – the camera script as worked out by the director and made sense of and distributed by the PA. Each camera operator will also have each of his or her shots detailed on individual camera cards (these are usually only used for complicated dramas), which will also be prepared by the PA. There is therefore less scope for creative decision making on the part of the studio camera operator; for the studio camera operator the real skill is applied in acting fast and getting the shot the director wanted first go.

When video camera crews go on outside broadcasts, their work is often similar to that in the studio as there is usually a van containing a mobile gallery in which the PA, director and vision mixer will be carrying out pretty much the same jobs that they would be doing back at the television station. The real difference comes with news or other types of action shooting, where often the camera operator can go off on his or her own and shoot what's required without the assistance of anyone.

GETTING THE JOB

Both the BBC and ITV run courses for camera operators, but these are difficult to get on to and current employees will always have priority. There are also a number of short privately run courses for camera operators, but these are generally aimed at people who are already in the industry.

There are, however, many colleges and universities which offer media courses with a practical element (see appendix A). Should you embark on one of these, you would be able to specialise in camera work, and build up a portfolio as well as gaining experience. Also, your course tutors should be able to put you in touch with television stations and production companies which might allow you to gain some experience by doing some unpaid holiday work (or paid work if you were lucky). Take all such opportunities, because particularly in small production companies, a keen, reliable and trustworthy person is a valuable commodity. If you've proved you are keen, reliable and trustworthy they might just feel it worthwhile to offer you some on-the-job training at some time in the future.

If a camera operator – and even a lighting assistant or LCO – is your goal, then you should be living and breathing cameras now. All forms of photography should be your passion; you should be experimenting with stills photography as well as video. Film cameras can be expensive, and the stock (and processing) certainly is, so it will be difficult for most people to be able to experiment with film. But again, some college courses and/or work experience might enable you to do this.

And then when the time comes for you to start applying for jobs – whatever your qualifications – don't be scared to start at the bottom. Being in the company of cameras and camera operators, learning about the equipment and the industry generally, will provide you with useful experience for the moment when you do write and ask for the job you really want to do.

And remember, all the time you are studying, or running for a production company – or even sweeping the studio floors somewhere – you should be using every spare hour you have taking your own photos, making your own videos, or offering your help (unpaid if necessary) to someone from whom you can learn.

As with pretty well any job in broadcasting, nothing helps you 'in' better than experience.

14

LOCATION, COSTUMES, MAKE-UP

These three areas of responsibility are lumped into one chapter because they all concern the 'look' and the 'feel' of a production. If you consider a period drama, particularly, these three elements must be very much in harmony. Yet in many ways the people responsible for these three areas on a production work in quite different ways. We'll begin with the locations manager.

LOCATION – WHERE TO FILM?

In the film sector, the job of finding the right locations at which the action will be based is often left to the production manager – who is effectively the producer's deputy. On a big-budget production there will be at least two people sharing this role, one of whom will be nominated locations manager.

In television a locations manager is only likely to be appointed on a major drama production. In such a case, the locations manager's first job will be to come to a thorough understanding of the script – first by reading it several times, and then by discussing it with the director, the producer, the writer and the script editor.

During these discussions, all the above will make their own suggestions as to the types of places which might suit the action – and the period, if the drama is not set in the present day. Only a certain amount can be decided at such meetings, however, and soon it will be down to the locations manager to start visiting places. On such visits, usually referred to as recces (short for reconnaissance), the locations manager will take photographs to give the director and others a general impression of the area. Also on the first recce the locations manager will check with local police and other key figures that nobody would object to filming being carried out in the area. If the locations manager takes a liking to one or more private buildings, permission to use them – inside or out – will be required by the owners. If the interior of a private house, shop or other such building is used, the owners will usually want payment. This, along with other factors such as transport facilities and any extra 'props' (such as trees, walls, period cars, replacement shop signs and street signs, etc.) must be considered by the locations manager in terms of the overall production budget.

Other factors to be considered include noise, light and the change of use of the location at different times times of the day. For example, the locations manager might one morning have found the perfect façade of a building for a particular scene, not realising that at 5.15 in the afternoon it becomes obliterated by rush-hour crowds coming from the nearby railway station. That same building might be in wonderful blazing sunlight for most of the morning, and in shade for the rest of the day. It might be directly beneath a flight path – which could cause noise, and possibly aircraft vapour trails which might not be in keeping were the production to be a period drama. All such considerations must be made before the locations manager decides on a particular location. For the next stage is to bring the director and possibly a camera operator or LCO back to the location, and if one of them discovers problems which the locations manager has failed to uncover, this will not only be a costly waste of time but also reflect badly on the locations manager.

Once locations have been decided upon, permissions sought, transport arranged and insurance and other technicalities taken care of between the locations manager and the PA, shooting can begin. Once shooting is underway, the locations manager might have a number of responsibilities – such as continued liaison between police and local authorities, or the owners of the buildings being used. And once shooting is complete, it will be the job of the locations manager to ensure that everything is left as it should be, and to ensure that anyone who did the production any favours is thanked and, if pre-arranged, paid.

COSTUME DESIGNER – DRESSING THE CAST

As with pretty well everyone else in the team (producer and scriptwriter excepted), the costume designer's work cannot begin without a script. A rough script will do, but personalities and period must be known about in some detail before the costume designer can begin to think about who wears what and why.

And for most costume designers that will still be barely enough. Once assigned to a production, the first thing costume designers will do is bury themselves in research. They will consult their own reference works, visit libraries and museums and where possible, get hold of video cassettes of past films and television programmes which have dealt with the same subject and/or, period.

When the script is firmed up, the difficult questions come for the director, producer and scriptwriter/editor. For example, if the script indicates 'a crowd', how big is that crowd? They all have to be dressed. And is it a crowd of peasants or a crowd of aristocrats? A big crowd has to be as properly and accurately dressed as a small crowd, and as the costume designer begins to point such things out to a director, producer and scriptwriter/editor (see chapter 16), so changes start to be made in order to reduce the costume budget.

A costume designer will often be the bearer of particularly bad tidings to director, producer and scriptwriter/editor. If, for example, the costume designer's research finds that the period written about actually passes through two, three or four changes in fashion, and that the principal characters would all be highly fashion-conscious people, this could up the budget considerably. A rewrite might be the only way around this, although all would resist this – for otherwise, what was the purpose of choosing the play in the first place?

Not all costume designers work on period pieces, of course. There are long-running drama series and soaps which are set in the present day and for which, in many cases, clothes can be bought off-the-peg. But even in such cases, costume designers bear a huge responsibility, for whenever a police officer, hospital nurse or member of the armed forces appears you can guarantee there'll be an army of experts among the viewing audience ready to pick up on inaccuracies.

Costume designers must also have a perceptive understanding of people and personality. For they will have to read a script and understand not just the period and class the various characters are from, but also the type of people they are – and must dress them accordingly. If a particular character is known to be some-

102

what introverted, then his or her costumes must reflect this. A costume designer's 'way with people' is also important when it comes to dealing with actors. For actors can be very temperamental people, and many will want to be seen only in the best light. If costume designers appear not to be sympathetic with the vanities of certain actors or actresses, horrible clashes can occur.

Costume designers must also have an understanding of lighting and stage design, as costumes can often clash with striking scenery and, in certain circumstances, their look can be totally altered by a particular type of lighting. Costume designers will rarely make the clothes which are worn on set, but merely research and design them and send them out for making.

During the production process the costume designers will often be on hand to be consulted on any related problems. There will also be dressers on hand whose job it will be to make minor alterations, to see that costumes are kept pressed and clean, and to help actors and actresses whilst dressing and undressing and during costume changes. This again is a job only for the understanding and tactful; dressers are often with actors during their most tense and pressured moments, and if they put a foot wrong can often be on the receiving end of vicious outbursts. For this reason dressers tend to be experienced, more senior people.

It is important to note that it is not only in dramas where costume designers are required; in variety shows they will often be required to clothe a whole dance troupe, while on a live Saturday morning children's programme – or a show like Channel 4's *The Big Breakfast*, for example – they might be required to ensure the presenters wear distinctive clothing. This may involve little more than taking the presenters shopping every few weeks. In the case of the high-profile, star presenter, a fashion designer of his or her choice might be called in to provide a new suit for every show. This would be exceptional and expensive.

MAKE-UP ARTIST

Apart from the dresser and occasionally the director in certain intimate scenes, it is generally the make-up artist who gets physically closest to the actors or personalities on a television production. This is a job which requires particular sensitivity, because more often than not the make-up artist is working at the crack of dawn with a nervous actor or presenter who might not have had a very good night, doing unspeakable things to his or her face and neck – and on occasions body – with cream, paint and towels.

It's a skilled and a creative job, but you will have to be a particular type of person to want to be in such an intimate situation with such potentially explosive people, day in, day out.

Again, the make-up artist's job on any production will start with the script. He or she will be looking carefully for directions which mention bright light, darkness, rain or wind or close-ups – particularly close-ups involving kisses. For bright lights or darkness will mean make-up will have to be adapted accordingly; rain or wind will affect face and hair; kissing and other intimate close-ups will mean extra care with facial blemishes and so on.

The make-up artist will also, like the costume designer, be looking for references to particular periods, and these will have to be researched. Also, like the costume designer, the make-up artist will be nagging the director or casting director for names (and ideally even photographs) of the actors or personalities involved in the production. Will they require moustaches? Will anyone need to be made to look bald, grey or 90 years old when the actor is in fact only 40? All such considerations require planning and on occasions the special ordering of equipment or effects.

If it is a wartime drama, will there be injuries? In such cases often specialist make-up artists are brought in with particular skills in this area.

Then there's the rather less dramatic work of the make-up artist, such as touching up the face of a politician before he or she goes on to a late-night news programme for an interview; or hiding the odd blemish on the face of a rock star before he or she goes on to play the interval slot on a talk show. This sort of make-up work is often called 'corrective' – in other words, the make-up artists are there to make good whatever is placed in front of them.

GETTING THE JOB: THE LOCATIONS MANAGER

Not a common job in television, the locations manager's job will often be carried out by a researcher (see chapter 15), PA or occasionally the production manager, director or even the producer.

The BBC and the larger ITV companies will have locations managers permanently on staff and will usually train new ones by attaching them to existing locations managers. Such attachments will generally be offered to people already employed by the company – researchers, for example.

Otherwise the locations manager's job is sometimes carried out by the production manager, a post which usually only exists in large film crews. The production manager is normally an experienced person who has worked his or her way up through the production team and has an understanding of all aspects of production. The production manager will often have certain management skills and might be experienced in law or financial management.

GETTING THE JOB: THE COSTUME DESIGNER

The costume designer will often be trained in fashion design or have general experience in the fashion business. An alternative route in is via art school. Some may have theatre training and background, and have spent much of their practical theatre experience working in the wardrobe department. Universities and colleges do offer courses in costume design as part of a broader arts, theatre or media qualification, and such courses would be invaluable to the would-be costume designer.

General qualifications would include an understanding of fabric types and textile design and a basic knowledge of dressmaking and the equipment used. As with pretty well all jobs in broadcasting, if you can gain some sort of work experience in any dressmaking or textile design environment this would help when you were applying for jobs or talking your way into the costume department in a film or television company.

Much costume design work is done on a freelance basis, and well-known and reliable designers will be in great demand by small production companies and television companies. Such freelancers will not confine themselves to television or film; pop video production companies and television and cinema advertisement producers always require costume designers and will provide lucrative work and a useful portfolio in times when the freelance television and film work is hard to come by.

GETTING THE JOB: THE MAKE-UP ARTIST

There will be some opportunity for training in make-up within the BBC and the larger ITV companies, but as with all training posts within these organisations, they are becoming fewer by the day and therefore tougher to get.

A simple route would be via regular training as a beautician and/or hairdresser. Such training would guarantee you certain qualifications which would provide a step-up – and a show of willing – when you went a stage further and applied to a television company or independent producer for work.

Some private film schools offer make-up courses, and art schools offer related courses – a qualification in sculpture would be useful, particularly if special effects make-up was your interest.

Whatever route you decide upon, a portfolio will help. If you do embark on a sculpture course, make sure there is a comprehensive photographic record of your best work – particularly any which you can photograph in an exhibition situation. And even if you do a regular beauty therapy and/or hairdressing course, make sure there is a photographic record of your achievements there.

Don't hesitate to put yourself forward as a make-up artist for any local drama groups you may come across. Sometimes simply having the equipment (which can be expensive and which you will have to consider as an investment in your future) and a little knowledge (plus perhaps a book which you can copy from at difficult moments) will be enough to get you in. Once in, make sure you get as much of your work as possible photographed and continue to apply for jobs at professional theatres and independent production companies at the same time. People will always be more sympathetic if you are currently involved in the sort of work you're applying for, even if it is unpaid and amateur.

After all, everyone has to start somewhere.

15

THE RESEARCHER

Researching a documentary series on the social history of China is rather different from researching a series of *Blind Date*. The researcher on the former might require a degree in history plus fluent Mandarin, whilst the researcher on the latter might simply need to be young, good looking, and have the eyes, ears and thick skin of a *Sun* journalist. It's unlikely that these two researchers' jobs would be interchangeable, and one researcher might be a graduate while the other might be rather less qualified.

The similarities between the two jobs would concern who they report to and the direct relationship between the research work they've done and the final product. In other words, although the researcher's job is not considered as prestigious as that of the producer or director, the researcher's work will invariably have a profound effect on the look and the content of any production. Here's how...

WHAT THE RESEARCHER DOES

The researcher's job is a great 'in' should you wish to become a producer or a director – or get even higher up the ladder. Greg Dyke, the multi-millionaire boss of the television division of the massive UK media company Pearson – which owns a number of television production companies and runs Channel 5 – was once a television researcher; so was presenter/writer/producer Jonathan Ross. So, a good job to go for. The trouble is, of course, that everybody knows it's a good job to go for.

So should you manage to secure a job as researcher on a particular production, you will really have to prove yourself, because there are a thousand others waiting in the wings to take your job should you mess up.

And while the job of researcher is most rewarding, allowing you to make your mark on a programme, it does also have its rather routine and unglamorous side, and it's here where you particularly have to excel. This is because the producer (to whom you will mainly report at the start) and the director (with whom you'll have more contact as the production develops) will warm fast to the researcher who can take the rough with the smooth; because the rough that you take as a researcher is usually that which would otherwise fall on the producer or the director!

To take the imaginary case of a documentary series of four half-hours on, say, four self-employed people, the researcher might come in before any such people have been found. And here's where the researcher must strive to avoid any resentment – for it might be he or she who finds the four perfectly fascinating subjects for the series, while the producer and director get all the credit. Yes, it could well be the researcher who is sent out to find the subjects for the series. And it is here, too, where ingenuity and creativity must be applied early. It would be very easy for the researcher to call upon four friends – say, a decorator, a freelance journalist, a car mechanic and an actor – and look no further. The likelihood that these would make good subjects for a documentary would be slim, and the fact that they just happen to be mates of the researcher would not reflect well.

No, in the case of our four-part series the researcher would do well to look in a number of directions – unlikely directions – and find a bunch of people who we in our ordinary lives might not often come across. A person who breeds snakes and hires them out for use in films, television programmes and theatre productions; a self-employed stripper; an inventor who, 99 times out of 100, has his inventions rejected; and a freelance after-dinner speaker: with such examples you're moving away from the rather dull idea of watching interviews with people who have bought a computer and a fax machine and work from home, and are moving towards something more unusual, more visually interesting – and, you will hope, something people might talk about at school, college or work the next morning.

At the start, then, the producer will have a vague – or not so vague – brief from the programme department head or from the commissioning editor. The producer will then work with the researcher and the director in order to firm up the ideas for the programme or series of programmes. If the producer is of the hands-off variety, he or she might leave a great deal up to the researcher at this stage; if, on the other hand, the producer is a control freak, the researcher might be left to very dull tasks like typing up the producer's reports, building up a book of contacts for the programme or series and arranging cars, train tickets and flights for members of the production team and guests. Even in the latter case, however, it is worth doing everything to the best of your ability – and with a smile on your face. Because at the end of it all, if the production has gone well, this is all that will matter to the producer, director and others, and they will recommend you – or re-employ you – almost as a matter of course. If, on the other hand, you have complained about being given all the boring jobs, however justified you may be, you will carry a black mark around with you and you might find that getting the next job will be more difficult.

Of course, the researcher's job will vary from programme genre to programme genre. On the documentary series on the social history of China, the researcher would be spending a considerable amount of time in museums, with his or her head buried in books, and a certain amount of time in China, gathering information, finding locations and finding people who are prepared, able and allowed to speak to camera.

Quite by contrast, the researcher on the gameshow would be spending most of his or her time finding people – for the audience and as guests. So many members of the public will volunteer to make fools of themselves on television; and so many more will jump at the chance to sit in the audience in a hot sweaty studio for the privilege of being able to watch members of the public make fools of themselves on television. These members of the public will write to the programme in their thousands, offering their services, and it will be the researcher's job to sort through this mail, decide which of it should be followed up and start to make contact with the people concerned.

Dealing with such people can be comparatively easy, because they all want to be involved. This job becomes less easy when you have to start telling people they're not wanted. Potential gameshow guests will have to look good on television and will have to be articulate, reasonably intelligent and trustworthy, and it is often the researcher's job to find those who have all these attributes, and to discard the rest. Many people are brought in for preliminary tests or 'auditions' for gameshows only to be told they can't be used.

Then there are the people whom you want to appear on television but who may be reluctant – in a probing documentary, for example. To be brought in as a researcher on a documentary about racism, for example, could be fraught with problems. Finding active racists – through the political parties and other organisations which expound racist views – wouldn't be difficult, and many of them will be more than happy to pump up their egos and publicise their contemptible cause by coming on television. To find victims of racial abuse or attack and to persuade them to speak might be harder, however. They might not want to be recognised for fear of reprisals; they might simply want to forget the whole episode and not bring it back to life by discussing it in front of the television cameras.

A researcher working on a documentary about a serious disease might have the unenviable task of persuading a sufferer – possibly bed-ridden – to discuss his or her situation on television. Such situations require sensitivity, tact, persistence and a certain amount of courage. Such work can be challenging, and ultimately satisfying – some documentaries can change things – but it is rarely for the faint-hearted.

Truly enjoyable research work might be found on a travel programme, a drama or a feature film. With travel programmes, however, budgets might require producers, PAs, production assistants or even presenters (if they're presenting a personal viewpoint of a place) to provide most of the research, the official job of researcher being dispensed with. Suffice it to say, however, that should you be offered the job of researcher on a travel series – which visits the Caribbean, southern Italy, the mountains of Colorado and the beaches of Bali – you are likely to be in for an amazing time. Researching a film or a television drama set in Venice in the seventeenth century would be a pleasant little number too. However, it is often the case that the scriptwriter and script editor will provide most or all of the research for a television drama, while in feature films, a true expert – who might have nothing to do with the film business at all – will often be brought in where really thorough research on a person, place or period is required.

Whatever the genre of programme, however, the researcher

will be expected to have provided all the answers asked by producer and director, and more, and often present it in a well-laid-out document, complete with the names, addresses and phone numbers of any contacts made during the research period.

JOURNALISTS

A different type of research is involved in the production of television news and magazine programmes – such as breakfast television, early evening news/magazine programmes and the big television news bulletins of the day.

The people who 'research' many of the stories featured in such programmes are usually called journalists or reporters and will carry out and present their research in rather a different way from that of the typical television researcher. Perhaps the most fundamental difference between journalist/reporters and researchers is that journalist/reporters' voices are often heard narrating their own filmed reports and occasionally they appear on screen. We will deal with the television news journalist in detail in chapter 22.

RESEARCHER: GETTING THE JOB

Television researchers are often graduates, and most graduates who aim for such a position in television will be aiming higher in the long run.

To be offered a research job you will have to show that you are lively, open-minded, bright, educated, full of ideas and enthusiasm and good with people. Prior work experience in journalism or radio would help; a producer would be pleased to know that you had experienced both a fraught newsroom and tight deadlines. Work in PR, or even in some non-media research position, would help too.

Once you have been offered a job, however short the contract might be (and three months is not uncommon), you will get more. But you'll have to keep on your toes. Try and make contact with as many producers and independent production companies as you can. Once you become known as personable and keen, with some successful experience, you'll find the work will start coming to you.

But it's getting the first job that will be hardest, and if you know that television research is what you want to do even whilst you are still studying at university or college (and don't forget a degree or similar qualification will help), then you are advised to start making contacts even before your course is over. Write to producers and production companies, tell them you want experience, and that you're prepared to do part-time work whilst still at college. Be honest, explain yourself well and make it clear that even if they can't offer you any actual work, you would be happy to 'shadow' a researcher (follow him or her around, do unpaid dogsbody, work etc.) just for the experience.

Or you could take a different route and become an expert in something. Perhaps you studied Chinese, a particular science or a particular country whilst at college; maybe you speak ten languages, have an encyclopaedic knowledge of Russian history or are the world's greatest living expert on classical music. One day your expert knowledge will come in handy to a producer working on a particular programme; all that you have to do is make sure that the producer knows you exist. This you can do by advertising in the trade papers (see appendix B), and writing to as many producers and production companies as you can (see appendix B). All sensible producers will keep such letters on file; and if you write enough times (sensibly – don't pester) you might well remain in the back of a number of people's minds. When, in future, your particular skill is required they might well remember your letters, or at least find them again in your files, and suddenly you're in demand.

And remember, particularly with the job of researcher, that the various initiatives you show in trying to get a job in the first place will help, as they will prove you have good ideas and are persistent.

16

THE SCRIPTWRITER

This is certainly not a job you aim for half-heartedly. If you want to be a scriptwriter (or screenwriter, as they are known in the film industry), it's because you know you can write, because you have stories to tell and because you sincerely believe that as many people as possible should hear and see them.

WHAT A SCRIPTWRITER DOES

In television fiction, the scriptwriter both puts the words into a character's mouth and decides what happens to him or her, on screen and off. The scriptwriter also decides what went on in that character's past and what will happen in that character's future. The scriptwriter chooses the type of language a character will use, whether or not that character is going to fall in love, with whom and when, and whether that love will last.

In a comedy the scriptwriter will set up a number of scenes designed to make us laugh, and will put jokes into the characters' mouths. In a soap opera the scriptwriter will decide how and where the characters interplay, and will devise the regular 'cliffhanger' or unfinished ending which leaves the audience desperate to watch the next episode.

In a factual programme – a documentary, for example – the scriptwriter does quite a different job. For he or she will be creating a narrative based on facts, usually laid out in programme research files, often spoken by a faceless voice (or voice-over) and guided by a series of pictures, the nature of which the writer can never fully control. With documentary, in many cases, the writer will also be the director or the producer – one of whom might have initiated the programme and therefore has strong views about the points which need to be put across and how they should be written.

In the case of an entertainment programme – say, a mix of comedy, music and dance – the writer (or usually the vast team of writers) will have the peculiarly disjointed job of writing short jokes, introductions and off-the-cuff comments for programme hosts and comedians, many of which are designed to sound as if they were never written by anybody.

Major television dramas are very often commissioned, or at least part-initiated, by a major broadcaster. The broadcaster might be part-funding (or co-producer of – see chapter 24) the drama and might therefore have the rights to broadcast it first – before it goes abroad, for example. In such a case, where the broadcaster initiates the work, it is likely that a writer will be approached by a producer and asked to write to a particular brief – or commissioned. This job would usually be done by a known, tried-and-tested person, in collaboration with producer and script editor; or sometimes a producer might approach a bright young playwright whose work is winning acclaim in the theatre, but who has yet to be proved on television. To commission such a writer can add a certain credibility to a production, and the producer is bound to be praised for supporting new talent.

Another way a writer can get such a writing job is to submit an idea to the commissioning editor at the drama department of the BBC, one of the ITV companies or a large independent producer which is well known by the BBC and ITV (or other broadcasters abroad) as a provider of drama. This idea would usually be presented, initially, as an outline of story and principal characters on just a couple of well-presented sheets of paper. If the producer was interested, he or she would ask the writer to develop the idea, and present a 'treatment', an extended outline of the drama which would flesh out the characters, the setting and the mood. If this were accepted a full script would be commissioned which would include all the dialogue and which, in collaboration with the editor, would become the 'shooting script', in other words, the one which would eventually be distributed to all cast and crew and to which would be added directions by the director. To achieve the final shooting script usually takes several rewrites, and it is here that the tact and skill of the script editor comes into play.

The writing of a major drama is usually something that comes to aspiring scriptwriters quite late in their career. There are other forms of writing for television where the responsibility can be shared and the writer's craft developed 'on the job'.

Soap operas, or long-running drama series, usually employ teams of writers, all of whose work is co-ordinated by the script editor and storyliner, with the help of a researcher. In such a 'writing team', different writers will have different strengths, and if all are working well together these strengths will be used to their advantage. For example, one of the writers might be particularly good at writing dialogue for men-in-the-pub or on-the-factory-floor – while another might be strong on setting up the more dramatic storylines involving illicit affairs, crime, unwanted pregnancies and the like. In an ideal situation these writers will be used according to their strengths, collaborating with each other and sharing the duties according to the instructions of the producer. In such a team the storyliner will develop the story and keep tabs on it, making sure it remains feasible, realistic and likely; the script editor, meanwhile, will serve as the liaison between the writers and storyliner and the producer. If the producer wants the soap to take a particular turn this will be relayed to the storyliner, who will work out how this could happen. This in turn will be relayed to the writers, who will make the characters make it happen.

Such experience is invaluable to a writer with the aim of going on to write major dramas, for example, as such long-running series are the perfect place to develop strengths, to identify weaknesses and to learn how producers and script editors function. To be on such a writing team (which also exist for sitcoms in the US, but less so in the UK) also allows one to see how other writers work, and this can boost one's confidence.

That's not to suggest, of course, that to be a scriptwriter on a long-running (and often high-rating) soap is anything like a trainee position. It's generally a well-paid, highly pressured and highly skilled job. But it's also a job that people would generally want to graduate from, unless, of course, they've reached this position at the autumn of their career.

THE MECHANICS OF SCRIPTWRITING

Exactly how a script is written is often hard to imagine for the layperson. A good script – a good drama script, at least – will offer such believable dialogue, sounding as if it came from people's mouths rather than from the pen (or the word processor) of a writer, that it's difficult to believe that those words were ever written down.

But it almost always is all written down. A drama script will be complete with dialogue – ifs, buts, umms and ahs, deep breaths, sighs, coughs, movements – the lot.

And all this has to be put on the page in a very precise manner. Film scripts, in particular, have to be written in such a way that a producer can instantly tell how long they are simply by looking at the stack of pages. Some can tell the length of the film literally by weighing the script. On a film script, the scene descriptions and character information are usually written right across the page, while the dialogue will be centred on the page, leaving wide margins at either side for the director's notes.

A television script is prepared in two columns, with the camera instructions and other notes related to the visuals in the left-hand column, and the dialogue and any sound effects and music detailed on the right. There was a time when this two-column-format script would have to be painstakenly prepared on a type-writer by the PA. Today, however, many production outfits will have a computer program which will format the script in this way for you. And if not all production outfits have this facility, all live television situations certainly will.

Most television scripts – particularly television drama scripts – take a long time to reach the final draft stage. This is because it's much cheaper – if laborious – to make as many changes and amendments as possible before the studio, equipment and crew have been booked. Once you're paying for studio and people time, any time wasted on rewrites is costly.

In a television documentary, the final script – to be spoken in voice-over or to camera – might well be worked on once a rough edit (see chapter 19) of the film has been done. This is because much of a documentary script must be written to the images the viewer will see on screen, and often it is not known what these are going to be until they are shot. Once they are, an editor will work on them with the director and shots will be selected in order to tell the story the director/producer wants to tell, or to tell the story which has emerged from the shooting. This is a far less formal way of writing for television, and the people who write such scripts are usually an integral part of the production

116

process – often they are producers or directors who have initiated the programme idea. Otherwise they are scientists or some other type of expert, with a passion; either they have managed to persuade a producer or broadcaster to make a programme about their passion, or they are known for their work, and have been approached by a broadcaster to help make a programme on their subject.

Such people might not be natural writers, and here a script editor plays an important role in advising what can be said and what can't. Again, tact and diplomacy on the part of the script editor are essential.

WAYS INTO SCRIPTWRITING

There is an increasing number of short courses in scriptwriting as well as scriptwriting units included in media degrees and film-school courses. But there is nothing like experience for getting you along in this area of the business.

What's important here is momentum. If you want to be a script or screenwriter (the latter is a term more used in the film industry, but increasingly film writers are contributing to prestige dramas and drama series on television as well as made-for-TV films), then the people whose door you'll be knocking on, day in, day out, will want to know that writing is what you do. So, if you've been a camera operator or a PA for the last five years, they'll be wondering why you haven't been trying to write any scripts. Where are your proven writing skills? Where is the proof that this is what you desperately want to do?

On the other hand, if you've been a journalist; an advertising copywriter; a small-time producer who also writes most of the scripts for the programmes he or she produces; a writer of radio drama; a short story/children's story writer; a novelist; a writer or director for the stage; anything which shows that writing – the stories, the characters, the words, the message – is what you're interested in, then you have a chance.

Radio has a good record for the nurturing of writers. There isn't a great deal of radio drama produced in the UK other than that which is broadcast by the BBC, but the BBC itself gets through over 1,000 hours a year. It doesn't pay well, but it has to be written and BBC Radio script readers – the people who look through the mountains of stuff sent in unsolicited – will rarely reject something simply because it is by an unknown. If screenwriting is really something you're keen on, then it is worth listening to the afternoon plays and other dramas which feature on BBC Radio (mainly Radio 4), getting to understand the sort of thing that works and trying to write to that style. Also get to know the names of the people who receive and assess any scripts which are sent in. If you can establish personal contact with people, even better.

Comedy is another route in. The early-to-mid-1990s have been a boom time for comedy in the UK – there hasn't been a great amount of new, innovative situation comedy on television, but many young stand-up comics have made names for themselves for inventive routines on stage, and if any of them make a name for themselves outside the cabaret rooms – on radio or as guest stand-up comedians on television – many producers are open to ideas about how to use them further on television.

Or you might want to try a more formal route – by signing with an agent. Agents are fussy, but they always want to keep their books full and have something to offer a producer if asked. If you present yourself well to prospective agents, always have something in your portfolio that you know will impress, and don't give up, one will bite eventually – if you're good.

And if you lose heart touting your wares around agents' offices (you will find a list of agents specialising in television in the annual *Writers' and Artists' Year Book*, published by A. & C. Black, and in the annual *Writer's Handbook*, published by Macmillan), then the Writers' Guild of Great Britain (see appendix B) could be of some use to you. Based in London, the Guild is a sort of trade union for writers and has done some good work in the establishment of industrial agreements for writers. It can provide help for members on contracts and holds regular workshops which can assist you in developing your craft. To gain full membership you will need to have written a novel, or a full-length television play (or something similarly prestigious), but lesser work can gain you points towards full membership and temporary membership – at around £50 for your first year – can help to give you the contacts you need to develop your career.

Clearly the job of script reader (whose job is to read through, and usually reject, the hundreds of unsolicited scripts received by broadcasters and independent producers) or script editor can lead to the possibility of having your own script accepted, but these jobs are also difficult to come by. Again, gaining the trust of the producer – and gaining his or her confidence in your literary, your editing and ultimately your writing skills – is the way in to both these jobs, and this is done by networking, in other words, making contacts in the industry as and whenever you can.

Otherwise, just get yourself published. Write a write book, a newspaper article, get a job as a journalist, send in unsolicited articles and ideas for articles to editors of magazines and news-papers. Once you're published, you're on your way. It doesn't have to be a novel – they're almost impossible to get published – but if drama is what you want to get into, then a few short stories sent off to a handful of publishers would be a start.

You're getting the idea, anyway, aren't you? That if you want to write for television, you've first got to write for yourself, and get to like what you write so much that it becomes easier and easier to persuade other people to like it too.

17

THE DESIGNERS

The set is, in effect, the four walls within which the performers in a television production – be they actors, presenters or entertainers – do their stuff. If it's a good set, the viewer often won't think about it, because it will be exactly right for its purpose, serving as the almost invisible framework within which the action takes place. If it's a bad set – looks cheap, fake or badly made – the viewer will notice and it will detract from the production. So you see, like the make-up artist and the costume designer, the set designers and builders have quite a reponsibility; and if they do their job badly they'll be noticed and criticised, and if they do it well they'll be ignored. By all except those in the know, that is . . .

SET DESIGNER, ART DIRECTOR, PRODUCTION DESIGNER, STYLIST: WHAT THEY DO

The above terms are tending to overlap these days, as the film and television industries are converging and as multiskilling becomes more common throughout the media. In the cinema, the person with overall responsibility for the design and look of the film might be referred to as the production designer; there might be an art director on the production as well; in a major television drama there might be somebody called the production designer working with an art director, but generally in television the set designer is the person with overall responsibility for the space in which actors or entertainers perform.

The term 'stylist' is used mainly in the production of pop videos and television and cinema advertisements and may refer to the person responsible for the total look of the production. In big advertising or video productions the stylist might work more on the decoration of the set and the people, while a set designer might be brought in for more complex design and structural work.

Once again, it depends on the dimensions of the production and, of course, budget, who is employed to do what in this area of production and what they are eventually called in the credits. For the purposes of this book, the set designer is the person responsible for the sets on the average television production.

The set designer will be brought in early on in the life of a production. If the programme in question is a historical drama, the set designer, like the costume designer, will be researching the architecture and trends in interior design of the period. And if the production requires both studio and location scenes, the set designer might well work closely with the locations manager on one of the pre-producton recces, simply to ensure that what is designed for the interior shots matches the exterior shots. In such cases the set designer might remain on hand throughout the shooting period simply to keep an eye on continuity.

At the start, the designer will be sketching floor plans and discussing them with producer, director and script writer/editor. These will be revised after various discussions, and eventually, the designer will have produced a set of accurate architectural drawings of the set which is to be built. The designer and director will also by this stage have produced a storyboard (which looks rather like a comic strip) depicting the various scenes and how the set would look in them. Radical changes must really be made at this stage if at all possible, because next, a scale model will be built and plans will be given to the workshops (which exist in-house at the BBC and the ITV companies but might be those belonging to outside contractors in other cases).

The scale model of the set will be used to check that cameras can go where they need to go, that it is practical for the actors and that no awful shadows will be cast by the lights hitting certain aspects of the set. So at this stage, the set designer will be collaborating with the director (and possibly camera crew) for information on where the cameras will be; with the costume designer to check that the design of the costumes doesn't clash with the design of the set; and with the lighting technician to ensure that set and lighting work in harmony.

With the set now being built – quite separately from the rest of the production process, by people working from plans rather than any knowledge of the script – the question of 'dressing' the set must be considered. This will often be done by design assistants working under the set designer. The job will involve choosing the materials for curtains; selecting floorings and wallpaper styles (which will often be painted on, as many period wallpapers are either seriously expensive or unavailable) and selecting props from the props department or seeking them out if the props department doesn't have them in store.

In a period drama getting the details right is crucial. Apart from the fact that a small number of irritating members of the great viewing public will write in to say if the type of cigarette holder used by the heroine in a 1920s period piece was not actually designed until the mid-1930s, it is important for the feel of a production that the details are right. Even if audience and actors are unaware of an inaccuracy, if something is wrong simply because it hasn't been properly thought out, then it will reflect generally on the production as a whole.

Of course, not all set designers work on period dramas. Consider some of the new-style television productions which are designed to reflect these times, in which much of the leisure time of children and young people is spent in front of computers, playing weird and wonderful fantasy quest games. Productions like *Gladiators* and *The Crystal Maze* (a British fantasy gameshow for young people) are staged in bizarre settings and represent quite a challenge both for designers and builders. Some productions will incorporate computer effects into actual sets; others will use electronic trickery to superimpose backgrounds where they don't actually exist in the studio. In such cases the designer must understand the technology being applied, and work in close collaboration with the people operating the special effects in order that they complement the set design and don't simply distract the viewer's attention from what the programme is really about.

Then there is the rather more simple set design of a talk show or a news programme. Simple these may be as far as we the viewers are concerned, but these sets also have to be gentle on the eye, create exactly the right atmosphere for the programme in question, and show the personalities concerned in the best light possible.

GRAPHIC DESIGN

Another element of a television programme which viewers often ignore altogether – unless it's very bad or very good – is the graphics. In the case of most productions, graphics only appear at the beginning and the end of a programme: at the beginning to introduce the programme by telling us what it's called and naming the key personalities; and at the end to tell us who did what – right down to the grip and the best boy (see next chapter).

In the past there has not been a great deal of work for graphic designers in television; where the media are concerned they have principally been in demand by television and cinema advertisement producers, corporate video producers and, more recently, pop video producers.

More and more now, however, television programmes – particularly magazine programmes and those aimed at a younger audience – use graphic sequences to break up the programme and identify different sequences within it.

The recent outbreak of new cable channels has also increased the workload for graphic designers specialising in television. MTV, the music channel which originated in the US but which now has headquarters all over the world, uses animated 'idents' which are designed to reinforce the 'brand name' of MTV throughout the day and night's broadcasting. These idents are changed and redesigned frequently, to help the channel give the impression that it's constantly moving with the times. In such cases, specialist graphics and effects 'houses' or production companies will be offered contracts to provide these graphic sequences. Such companies might offer dogsbody work to young graphic design students eager to get into this aspect of the business. They might also recruit from magazines and non-broadcast, non-film design studios.

GETTING THE JOBS

Set designers will generally have a degree in some area of design – architecture, interior design or stage set design. Some may find their way into the business through a particular type of expertise – in antiques, in the history of architecture or as a draughtsperson. It's quite common now for designers to be taken on directly from college or university courses. This is because you don't always need to be experienced at the job itself to be able to prove you can do it: if you have a talent for design and drawing, it will show itself early on, and you won't have to spend time nurturing that talent.

What a young set designer won't necessarily have is the business skills required in the job. As with all areas of television production, set designers are guided as much by budget as inspiration, talent and a fine script. The skilled businesslike designer will have cost on his or her mind at all times, and it will constantly affect decisions. In simple terms, if it doesn't have to be 'in shot' it won't cost anything. The fired-up young designer might feel that for artistic reasons and truth to the script real marble should be used to create the pillars at the doorway for the entrance on to the scene of a particular nobleman; the budget-conscious designer who has been doing it for years might, in collaboration with the director, shoot the character's entrance in close-up, or avoid the scene altogether.

Work as a design assistant can serve as a good step up to the job of set designer, but qualifications will be important here, too. Work in the set-building workshop can be won simply by having skills in carpentry, or general building skills, or experience perhaps as a shop fitter; while the props department would be happy to employ people from the theatre. There is no natural progression from the set-building workshop or props department to the job of set designer; you would have to be working for some time with small teams and have won the confidence of set designers and producers for anything like this to happen.

Graphic designers will have specialised in graphic design at art school. And to repeat a point made earlier, you prove your artistic ability whilst at art school, so end-of-year shows and any other contacts you can make with potential future employers will be crucial if you want to find employment in your chosen field as soon as your college or university education is complete. And if you don't go into some kind of work – or at least try to – pretty soon after qualifying, future employers are going to want to know why.

Don't forget that design appointments in film or television are not made lightly; after all, the look of a film or television programme is crucial to its success. No producer or television company is going to sacrifice that look by employing anything but the best.

18

THE TECHNICIANS

Lights, camera, action! This well-worn phrase signifying that filming can commence takes into consideration a couple of the technical areas involved in a production – lights and cameras – but ignores the sound crew and several other crucial people along the way. Maybe the phrase was first coined in the silent era. Whatever, there are many more technical jobs to be done before anyone has the right to shout 'Action!'.

LIGHTS!

These are set up by electricians, often referred to as lighting technicians or 'sparks'. Their responsibility is generally for the electrical safety and faultless functioning of the equipment, rather than for its creative use. The creative decisions as to where the lights go and what their functions are will have been made in advance by the lighting director (see chapter 13); the lighting technicians will then wire and set up the lights according to the lighting director's plan.

The lighting technicians will work under the immediate direction of the chief lighting technician or 'gaffer', as he or she is referred to in the film business. Under the gaffer is the second electrician (or in films, the 'best boy') and then as many lighting technicians or electricians as the production requires.

Lights are usually attached to a lighting grid, which is a criss-cross of iron bars hung high over the studio floor. There will be occasions when they'll be attached to upright poles which stand on the ground – these are used more on outside broadcasts and location shoots, as occasionally are small, hand-held lights with which the lighting technician will illuminate a specific object – a character's face, for example. Lights are also, occasionally, attached to a specially built tower of scaffolding, or a single mesh of metal bars which hangs high over the studio floor, known as a gantry.

Wherever the lights are attached, they are heavy, and usually require the technician to do some climbing. Some lighting grids can be lowered so that all the lights can be attached before the grid is raised back to its required height; others remain higher than most people would ever wish to be climbing, especially carrying a heavy light encased in metal. Important qualifications for a lighting technician, then: strength and a head for heights.

With the lights safely bolted on in their correct places, one or two technicians will be required to remain during the production for safety and maintenance reasons. When the broadcasting unions governed the size of a production team there would have been more hanging around during a production 'just in case' than you will find today. But technicians will always be required to be around after the bulk of their setting up work has been done, for should a light blow, or turn out to be misplaced, it would be the technician – possibly the gaffer or someone acting on the gaffer's instructions – who would have to rectify the situation.

Once 'Action!' is underway, the lights will be controlled from the lighting gallery (which may or may not be a part of the gallery from which the director operates) by the lighting director and an assistant.

SOUND

Sound is another element of a production which the viewer takes very much for granted. Yet most programme soundtracks are a complex mix of sounds, which have often been recorded separately and mixed by a highly skilled sound dubbing editor, in order that voices, background noise and music can work together in harmony, without one drowning out the other.

In a studio situation, the sound will be balanced and controlled by a sound supervisor up in the gallery, who will sit at a console and mix together the various sound sources whilst shooting is in progress. These sounds might be coming from the actors on the studio floor (in the case of a drama); from the 'grams' operator, who feeds usually pre-recorded sound effects and music through to the console as and when the script requires; and occasionally from a studio audience, in the case of a situation comedy, game-show or talk show, for example.

The voices and movements of the actors in a studio-based drama will often be picked up by microphones hanging down below the lighting grid. There may also be boom microphones (mikes on long sticks pointed at the relevant sound source) and gun microphones (directional mikes which can pick up sound from specific sources by aiming like a gun directly at the source) operated by sound technicians out on the studio floor.

The boom mike is a crucial tool for programmes in which the studio audience participates, and where each person could not possibly be wired up with his or her own 'lapel mike'. The lapel mike – so-called because it's usually attached to the lapel of a guest (or in the lapel area if there isn't a lapel!) – is designed so that the speaker can be heard without having a microphone rammed down his or her throat. It is particularly useful for people who are not used to studio situations.

Generally, once a lapel mike (or a ceiling-hung mike) is positioned there is no need for a sound technician unless something goes wrong. So a technician will usually be on hand just in case a lapel mike drops off or a mike cable becomes unplugged or breaks. Otherwise, in a studio situation most of the microphones will be controlled at the mixing console, by the sound supervisor.

On location, the sound crew will comprise a sound operator (often identified as the boss by the name sound supervisor) and a crew of sound technicians. On a small production one supervisor and a technician might be enough; on a major drama or a feature film the sound crew might require a considerable number of people to be on hand.

The sound operator on location often appears to be working out of step with the rest of the production team. This is because, whilst everybody else's attention is usually on the actors (in a drama) or the subject being interviewed (in a documentary or a news report, for example), the sound operator might be concentrating on something quite different. This is because, with the headphones on, he or she can often hear things that nobody else will notice. On one shoot I was on, the camera crew and director were getting very irritated by the sound operator, who would not allow shooting to go ahead until he could work out where a rattling noise he could hear was coming from. Nobody else was aware of this noise, but the sound operator was combing the area to find the noise's source. He eventually found a roadside power generator to which was attached a pneumatic drill complete with operator, pounding a hole in a nearby road. The workman was asked to stop for five minutes, and the shoot went ahead. Had the sound operator not detected this sound it would have turned up on the soundtrack and it would have been necessary to shoot the sequence again.

Such are the required skill and patience of the sound operator – on location particularly. And he or she is not going to be thanked for delaying a shoot in this way, unless the reason for the delay is eventually made clear to all. So an element of diplomacy and cool-headedness is also a requirement for a sound operator.

Also on location there will be a sound technician, whose job will be to do anything the sound operator is unable to do – such as hold a boom or a gun mike, check recording levels, run off and divert a parent with a noisy child if they suddenly approach the area, and generally keep a second pair of ears on what's being recorded.

With film as opposed to videotape, the sound is recorded separately from the image, on to magnetic tape using a reel-to-reel tape recorder. This means that the sound operator can work with some independence from the cameras – although, as explained in chapter 13, the soundtrack must be synchronised with the film at the start of each scene by use of a clapperboard. The tape will then be lined up with the film at the editing stage and cut with the film as editing takes place.

With video cameras, sound and image are recorded together on to one piece of tape. This means that the sound operator's monitoring and recording equipment is connected by cable to the camera, and so sound operator and camera operator become very much a close-knit team. For this reason many freelance location camera and sound operators like to travel as a team. You employ one; you get the other. This can make you more employable as a sound or camera operator, because the producer will only have to make one call to get both members of the team.

When all is shot and the editing process begins, the sound dubbing editor will have the often hugely complex task of cleaning up the soundtrack so that it runs smoothly from the beginning to the end of the programme. This might involve cutting out the sound of a roaring motor car from a particular sequence; cutting out the 'ums' and 'ahhs' from the interviewer's questions or the interviewee's answers; 'balancing' the tone of the voices or background noise so that it is even throughout; and weaving in music and sound effects so that they mix comfortably with the rest of the soundtrack.

ENGINEERS

As the jobs become more 'technical' so they begin to seem less glamorous, and certainly, in the eyes of the viewing public they become almost invisible. Your average couch potato knows roughly what a director does and is vaguely interested; your average couch potato might occasionally consider the difficult conditions under which camera operators work and what a fine job so many of them do. But when it comes to lighting technicians, sound operators and certainly engineers, that's where the lay-person tends to stop thinking about what goes into the making of a television programme. Yet without the engineers, there wouldn't be any television programmes.

Engineers work in a number of areas, but basically their reponsibilities lie with the technical facilities which enable a television station to broadcast programmes. They maintain the equipment which records and plays back programmes; they maintain the lines which bring programme feeds into the station and which send them out; they maintain the control room equipment, the studio facilities, the mixing desks and the monitors.

A key job of the engineering team is to ensure that a perfect video image is both recorded and transmitted. This is because, according to the terms of the licences granted by the government to the BBC and – through the ITC – the ITV channels, strict technical standards must be adhered to or penalties can be applied. Engineers are therefore required to ensure that these standards are always met. The vision controller, for example, will work in the gallery with the lighting director to monitor the quality of the image which comes from the cameras. These images must be properly colour balanced and properly exposed and there mustn't be any radical difference between the quality of image from camera to camera.

Engineers also work in the department known as VT or VTR (which stand for videotape or videotape recording). VTR is where all studio programmes are recorded and played back for transmission. It is where video inserts such as news reports are played into live or as-live programmes, and it is also where feeds from other broadcasting centres are brought in, monitored and recorded.

Outside broadcast engineers will carry out similar tasks, but the production team will be more dependent on the OB technician for the repair of equipment which has suddenly broken down on location. Back at the television station spare equipment would probably be on hand to replace broken equipment which could be repaired later; on location it's not easy to carry two of everything, so the engineer becomes a more crucial part of the team.

In the broader picture, engineers will install new equipment as old equipment wears out or becomes obsolete; and will assess new technologies and help the station adapt to them. In the case of new technology – for example interactive television (see chapter 25) – a senior executive might ask an engineer or engineers to assess it in financial and practical terms and provide a written report which would include the engineer's opinions on whether such equipment should be installed, and if so, when, and how much investment and training would be required.

Working beneath the engineers will be the technical assistants – often serving as trainee engineers – and the more junior technical operators. The assistants will often maintain equipment and generally fill in for the engineer at particular times, while the technical operators will be more involved in the preparatory work and the 'clearing up' jobs – such as ensuring that equipment is fully operational before use and safely 'powered down' and stored away afterwards.

GETTING THE JOB: THE LIGHTING TECHNICIAN

If television lighting technician is your goal, then first you must gain a sound electrical qualification, such as a City & Guilds certificate from a college of further education (see appendix A). Having achieved your qualification, you will need to make immediate moves towards the broadcasting industry in order to prove to future employees that this is what you want to do.

Write to everybody – the BBC, the ITV companies, BSkyB, cable companies such as MTV – any company you know which has its own studios and makes its own programmes (see appendix

B). You might also want to write to companies which hire out television studio facilities to independent producers (see also appendix B). Such companies might employ permanent engineering staff and may take on trainees.

Also, write to theatres – professional and amateur. For the professional theatre provides a perfect background for work in broadcasting. Working with an amateur dramatics group might help you while you wait to be accepted into a job in broadcasting. For even if you have not had any previous theatrical or broadcasting experience, a future employer would be impressed to see that you were indulging your passion in the evenings – and unpaid! – while you waited for your big break.

GETTING THE JOB: THE SOUND OPERATOR

Qualifications in electronics and/or science, maths or physics will help you towards a job on a sound crew. A big organisation like the BBC or one of the ITV companies would want more formal qualifications, while if you were to talk your way into a camera/ sound crew of the type described earlier, as a low-paid helper just to try you out, perhaps, your personality, reliability and trustworthiness might be as important as your qualifications in securing further, more lucrative work with that crew or with others to which they might recommend you.

Or, try getting onto a production as a runner. It can sometimes seem that the runner's job is the gateway to big-time success in all areas of the film industry and television; that is, of course, not true. But as I have stressed, and will continue to stress throughout this book, this industry is all about contacts, being trusted and being liked. Skills will come if you're keen and prove your aptitude. So, often people will take on a less skilled person because of his or her personality, willingness to learn and pleasant approach to teamwork.

This is not to say that qualifications and experience don't count. In sound, as with lighting, it might well be worthwhile volunteering to operate the simple sound equipment used by your local amateur dramatics society. This would prove not only how keen you were to gain relevant experience, but also that you were particularly keen to work in the performing arts. Add such experience to some good qualifications earned as early as possible in your career and you are on the right route.

GETTING THE JOB: THE ENGINEER

Qualifications in electronics, engineering or telecommunications – or all three – are essential to such work. A City & Guilds qualification or a degree in engineering or electronics would be more than adequate.

As a technician you will need at least up to A-level in maths and/or physics, and both technicians and engineers are increasingly using computers to aid them with their work – and maintaining computers, which are increasingly becoming a crucial element of the broadcasting industry.

Engineering is one area of broadcasting where you are not likely to get a job simply because you're a friendly, personable, honest sort of a person willing to try your hand at anything. All that will help, but your skills and knowledge are crucial here – to the safety of the people around you, and to the smooth running of the equipment.

19

THE EDITOR AND THE VISION MIXER

The editor and the vision mixer are the two people responsible for physically preparing the images we see for the screen. They have control over what order the pictures come in, and how long they remain on the screen. Yet their jobs are entirely different in the sense that the editor works to some extent alone, while the vision mixer works almost entirely on the instructions of the director and PA.

THE EDITOR

The editor's job is crucial in determining the look, the sound and the feel of the finished product. In film and video, it is very much the editor whose creative skills determine both the pace of the production and the way in which the sounds and images hold together and relate to each other, and to the audience.

In the film business, the term 'director's cut' has come to describe the re-edited version of a film which has already been released. This is partly a response to the increasing involvement of the producer – and even the executive producer – in the final version of a film. For while in film it is traditional that the editor works with the director (some directors – notably the infamous Michael Winner – edit their own films) in putting the film together, the producer's involvement is increasing, certainly in Hollywood. This is so that certain Hollywood 'trademarks' can be stamped on to the film, the producer believing that to succeed a film must take a certain course, be of a certain length, etc., etc. Directors, being forced to take a back seat in this way, are increasingly recutting films – creating the director's cut – to show what they really meant when they were making the film, and of course, they hope, to extend the film's commercial life as well.

But back to the editor, whose job is actually to make the cuts and the joins. Whether with film or with videotape, the editor's responsibility is to ensure that the production moves from image to image and scene to scene in a way that makes sense to the viewer, and in a way that makes sense of the story or subject matter which has been filmed. The final edit need not be so smooth that the cuts are invisible to the human eye: it may be decided that cuts should be sudden and dramatic, to jolt the viewer out of his or her complacency or to give the production a certain sense of drama. The smooth style of editing designed to make scenes flow into one another in order that the viewer thinks only about the narrative, the look and style, and not about the film-making process, is sometimes referred to as 'invisible editing'; this is the favoured style of much of the output of US television, particularly the glossy series which used to come out of that country but which have faded in popularity in the 1990s.

The editor often has to make tough decisions too, omitting seemingly important scenes because they simply don't sit comfortably in the sequence for which they were shot. Sometimes only the editor can know that a certain shot or scene won't fit even before trying, but often has to go ahead and put it into the rough edit just to convince a doubting producer or editor that he or she was right in the first place. It's a difficult job, because you're tampering with someone else's work. And it's not just the producer or director who can get upset by certain cuts: an actor's role can be seriously reduced by the merciless editor; a whole set, designed and built with passion to the last detail by the designer, can be dismissed by one ruthless cut with the editor's knife. So, aspiring editors be warned: the editor may often be the person who is responsible for making a passable product out of what would otherwise have been a dog's dinner, but more often than not, the editor's work will go unnoticed, and will win little praise and possibly even abuse from those who feel aggrieved by his or her actions.

EDITING FILM

There is a fundamental difference between film editing and videotape editing. Film is shot frame by frame, each frame being a single, complete picture recorded as the camera shutter opens, exposes the raw film stock briefly to light, and then closes again. So a complete film is made up of millions of single frames which, when projected rapidly one after the other, create the illusion of movement.

The physical job of editing is therefore comparatively easy, because there is a clean line between each image. When you want one shot to end and another to begin, you simply cut the first piece of film at the end of the last frame required and the second piece of film at the start of the next frame required and join them together – with tape, or sometimes glue. So, the actual cutting and joining process requires only basic skills and fairly simple equipment. If you appreciate, however, that a ten-second sequence in a completed film could feature ten, twenty or even more cuts, you begin to see where the real skill is required on the part of the film editor.

For example, a sequence in which a man walks along the street, stops at a doorway, turns to look behind him, puts a key into the keyhole, turns it, opens the door and walks into the building might last a total of 10 seconds. It could, however, include the following shots:

- Long shot of subject walking down street towards door
- Close-up of subject's face to establish subject's mood
- Back to long shot as subject stops at doorway
- Close-up of subject's head as it turns to look over left shoulder
- Point-of-view shot behind subject's left shoulder
- Close-up of subject's head as it turns to look over right shoulder
- Point-of-view shot behind subject's right shoulder
- Close-up of subject's hand with key as it moves towards keyhole; key turns
- Mid-shot of subject pushing open door
- Shot from inside hallway as subject comes through doorway from outside

Ten shots in all for a short sequence possibly lasting only around 10 seconds. And the final shot, filmed inside (possibly in a studio mocked-up as the interior of the building shot from the outside), will have been filmed days, possibly weeks, before or after the other shots. So here the editor not only has to cut a number of separate pieces of film so that they join seamlessly together into one piece of action; he or she also has to co-ordinate and keep track of hundreds – often thousands – of strips of film.

Usually this business of co-ordinating endless miles of film falls to the assistant editor. The assistant will match up the film with the soundtrack as they come in from their respective sources (film from the film processing laboratory, sound from the sound transfer laboratory), cut them into manageable lengths (usually around 30 metres) and carefully label them, indicating the name of the production, the film reel number and any other information provided by the production assistant or the laboratories.

When the editing process begins, the editor and director will work through the film, with one eye constantly on the shooting script, and put them roughly into order. This stage is called the 'rough assembly' stage. The cuts will then be 'tightened', in other words, frames will be removed in order to smooth out the scenes and bring the action closer into line with how it will be in the final edit: this stage is known as the 'rough cut'. The rough cut will then be trimmed down into a 'fine cut' or 'finished edit'.

At this stage the soundtrack will have been edited to match the images, but the sound editor will then have to add music and other effects. Once the soundtrack is finished, both sound and the edited film go back to the laboratories for a 'combined' print to be produced: in other words, a copy of the final edit and the synchronised sound combined on to one print.

The film editor works on a large machine through which the film and the soundtrack are run. The machine is usually equipped with foot pedals to stop and start the film, and cutting and 'splicing' equipment for the actual job of cutting and rejoining the film.

EDITING VIDEOTAPE

Although the videotape editor and the film editor are carrying out a similar job as far as the finished product is concerned – in other words, making sequential and narrative sense out of a string of initially unrelated shots – they work with quite different processes.

Videotape does not record images frame by frame. Rather, it magnetically picks up a series of electronic impulses which, when played through a VTR, are decoded and transferred into images.

Videotape cannot be cleanly cut like film; it is therefore edited in a different way.

The videotape editor does not physically cut tape. Instead, the required shots will be recorded, in sequence, from the original piece of tape on to a second piece of tape, which will eventually contain the complete edited programme.

To assist this process, all professional video cameras will have a facility which allows a 'time code' to be recorded on to the tape. This code – which identifies each video 'frame' in terms of hours, minutes, seconds and frame number – is usually recorded on to an audio track which can then be decoded by a time code reader in the editing machine. Specific edit points can then be noted down according to the time code reading so that accurate edits can be made when the final 'on-line' edit takes place.

You will often have heard or seen the terms 'off-line' and 'on-line' in the context of videotape editing. You could replace them with the film editor's terms 'rough assembly' and 'fine cut'. In many situations, the editor will make a rough or 'off-line' edit by simply recording material from the original master tape on to a VHS tape, and record from that VHS tape on to another VHS tape just to get – and to give – a rough idea of how the finished product is going to look. This might be done where the editor has gone on location in order that rough edits can be made on site. This may be necessary if the programme has to be edited quickly for broadcast on return from a few days' shooting away from base. Off-line edits might also be done in cases where the producer and/or editor won't be present for the final on-line edit. Once director and/or editor have approved the off-line version, they then know that an editor they trust will simply perfect it, without need of their attendance, at the on-line stage.

Off-line editing can save money, for many 'creative' decisions can be made outside an expensive on-line editing suite. Off-line editing also means that the precious master tape isn't continually being run back and forth while crucial creative decisions are made.

From the off-line edit, an 'edit decision list' (EDL) can be created which can then be taken into the on-line edit suites. In some cases the final edit can be done 'blind', in other words, by simply going by the time codes on the EDL and paying no attention to the images. And in highly sophisticated on-line suites, the EDL could be delivered on disk and the disk loaded into the machine to do the editing pretty well automatically.

With the arrival of digital technology an edit can now be done using no videotape at all. Digital editing, of course, means that precious time can be saved by not having constantly to wind and rewind videotape. Editors will have to keep track of new technology and make every effort to become familiar with it as soon as it is adopted by the industry. Otherwise, they can be left behind and find that all their work is being taken by younger people who adapt more easily and quickly to new technology.

EDITING: THE JOB

As an editor you need a sharp eye and a highly organised mind. You also need tact, in order to be able to tell someone clearly but kindly that the particular shot or scene they love 'has to go'; and you need patience. Because the job of editor requires long hours spent behind closed doors, watching the same few shots over and over again, trying to work out just how they should be cut together.

The editor on a particular production might work entirely alone, with producer and director happy that all will be done to their liking. On other occasions the editor might end up working with a director who perhaps once was an editor and can never quite leave the job behind.

All editors will, from time to time, find themselves in a situation in which the joining of two scenes seems impossible. Maybe the linking shot which was supposed to sit comfortably between them went wrong or just didn't come out. The creative, successful – and most sought-after – editor will work and work until some ingenious solution to the problem materialises. Maybe a brief cut to an indiscernible close-up coupled with some distracting sound will sort out the problem; maybe a few frames taken from some unrelated, but highly appropriate, shot might smooth the join. Get a director or producer out of a sticky situation in this way and you could find yourself in work for life. But how do you find the work in the first place?

GETTING THE JOB

The majority of people who become editors will have been taken on by broadcasters or facilities houses as trainees or assistants. It is possible to gain fairly comprehensive training as an editor at some film schools and colleges and as part of a degree in film and television or the media (see appendix A), but again, there are still far too few formal training courses which guarantee you work at the end of them.

Established freelance editors will always want a personable and trustworthy assistant to work with, and it is worthwhile writing to a number of them, explaining what experience you have and what your ambitions are. (Find the names and contact addresses from BECTU – see appendix B.) If you can, put together your own showreel of material you have edited yourself; shoot your own Super-8 film or videotape and edit it just to show a prospective employer what you can do. Super-8 editing equipment is very cheap, and rough video editing can be done from VHS recorder to VHS recorder. Another way to build up a portfolio of work would be to join a community video project, or find a local drama group or sports centre which makes its own videos for whatever purpose. If such a place has just the most basic of recording and editing equipment, you'll be surprised what a creative mind can do with it.

It's important to bear in mind that many people in the business believe that good editors have a natural feel for the job; that it's less about training and experience and more about being able to sense what's a good edit and what isn't. A portfolio – or showreel – of work demonstrating your 'editor's sense' will therefore be of great value to you.

Bear in mind, too, that editing equipment is becoming increasingly complex – computerised and digitised. This does not mean it is becoming harder to use, but it does mean that a more computer-literate mind might be more adaptable to new equipment than someone used to the old steam-driven machines. You, the bright young computer-literate person with the impressive showreel demonstrating your editor's sixth sense, might contact someone for a job just on the day when he or she has been reading about the latest digital, computer-aided editing equipment and wondering how on earth it can be mastered. You might be just the assistant this person needs!

THE VISION MIXER

The vision mixer is effectively an editor who operates in real-time. It is a television job and there is no equivalent in film. During the recording of a television programme, the vision mixer sits in the gallery at the director's side in front of a vast bank of monitors underneath which is a vast console of switches and faders. On these monitors can be seen what the cameras are filming; any VT inserts which might be needed for the production in question; outside broadcast feeds; satellite feeds; graphics; and so on.

On the instructions of the director the vision mixer will switch – or fade – from feed to feed, thus providing the required images for the production in progress. In the case of a pre-recorded programme these feeds will be being recorded by the VT engineer for future broadcast; and in a live situation, they will be going out live to every television set in the land.

So, it's a pressured job. The vision mixer's timing has to be immaculate; he or she has to be alert (in order to be able to watch a number of monitors at the same time whilst listening to the director's instructions) and calm.

In the case of a programme where images are cut to the beat of a piece of music, the vision mixer should at least have a sense of rhythm, if not greater musical skills. In comedy, a sense of comic timing would be useful. Although supposed to take strict orders from the director, a vision mixer can often cover up for an incompetent director – or one who simply isn't functioning very well on a particular day – possibly by catching a shot the director fails to notice or perhaps by going late to a shot which the director has requested unaware that it was not quite in focus, for example. The job requires the ability to anticipate and interpret the director's orders.

Some vision mixing desks will incorporate special effects buttons which the vision mixer might be required to operate. Particularly complex special effects are more likely to be added on afterwards in post-production, often by a specialist facilities company.

GETTING THE JOB

Most film and television courses at college and university will touch upon the vision mixer's job – and will give you the chance to have a go. A formal vision mixer's qualification does not exist, however.

It's a job that's taken by young people of both sexes (it's not dominated by one or the other), and vacancies are often filled from inside. So, any 'in' on the production side at the BBC, one of the ITV companies, BSkyB, a cable company such as MTV or a facilities house could lead you to the job of vision mixer if you show willing. A secretarial position, as long as it offers contact with production, would be a good start.

The vision mixer who shows initiative stands a good chance of being able to move on – to the position of PA or even, eventually, editor. Remaining calm under pressured live conditions in the gallery can say a lot about how you might perform in other jobs. Many don't simply see the vision mixer's job as a step up, however, but as an important and enjoyable position in itself.

20

TELEVISION: THE PERSONALITIES

Tell the uninitiated – the ignorant layperson – that your ambition is to go into television, and they will immediately conjure up an image of you sitting behind a desk reading the news, or on a breakfast television sofa interviewing somebody about their latest book. Because to so many, the personalities are television. They are what they see on the screen, day in, day out. And the programmes are made to look so slick that it doesn't occur to most viewers that while the programme they're watching is going on (or was being recorded) there are 101 people (see the last 11 chapters) working flat out to ensure that those personalities are seen in the best possible light.

Yes, it's so often the personalities who get all the credit, simply because they are the ones who get seen on the screen. To be fair, much of that credit is due. After all, to come across well on television is not easy. But then by the time most television personalities have actually made it in front of the camera for the first time, they've done the really hard bit – getting the job in the first place. Because it's not easy.

THE PRESENTER

The term 'presenter' refers to the person who fronts a programme – plays 'host' both to the programme guests and to the viewers at home. Presenters host chat shows; presenters host gameshows; presenters host breakfast television shows; presenters host consumer advice programmes. In most cases this is a highly prestigious job, and most presenters get paid very well for what they do. But strangely, in many cases the presenter didn't set out to be a presenter.

Taking a random sample of well-known and reasonably well-known television presenters, you can see how this strange breed of person comes from varied of walks of life. Jools Holland, presenter of music programmes on Channel 4 and BBC2, came to prominence as a musician. He still is a musician, but many people today know him better as a television personality. Paula Yates, who began her television career co-presenting with Jools Holland Channel 4's 1980s pop programme *The Tube*, started out as a journalist; she also gained notoriety as the girlfriend of pop star Bob Geldof. Cilla Black, presenter of gameshow *Blind Date* for ITV's station London Weekend Television, started out as a pop singer; Chris Evans, a leading presenter in both television and radio, started out as a studio assistant on a local north of England radio station; Noel Edmunds, too, started in radio; Clive Anderson, who has presented travel programmes, a gameshow and a talk show, started out as a barrister and part-time comedy scriptwriter; tennis television commentator and presenter Sue Barker, and her late colleague Dan Maskell, were professional tennis players; political programme presenters-cum-journalists Matthew Parris, Brian Walden and Peter Jay were politicians first.

The above are all British examples, and strangely the job of presenter rarely travels abroad. Exceptions who prove that rule are Jools Holland, who has presented a successful music programme in the US; and French television personality Antoine de Caunnes, who has fronted two successful cult programmes for Channel 4 in the UK, the music programme *Rapido* and the aptly named style-meets-comedy magazine programme *Euro-Trash*.

There are serious political programmes fronted by former newspaper journalists; there are light entertainment programmes fronted by singers, comedians and all-round entertainers; some former actors find their way into presenting jobs; well-known chefs or writers of recipe books often end up presenting cookery programmes; while most of the popular science programmes on television have been hosted by popular scientists. So how do you become a television presenter? One answer is: be a success in something else first!

There are no rules about how one might set about getting the job of presenter and no rules about the presenter should do the job. A presenter's job varies from programme to programme and from personality to personality. Most will be following scripts (even those who don't appear to be), but their level of involvement in the preparation of those scripts will vary enormously. A breakfast television presenter who might be working live in the studio (though not always on camera) for up to two hours will probably rely very much on research material provided and mugged up before the show, and perhaps a little the night before; the teleprompter (a machine which displays the presenter's script right next to the camera so it looks as if he or she has learned it by heart); and an earpiece through which the director and/or PA can feed directions, late information and other helpful last-minute pieces of information. The former-scientist presenter of a science programme, on the other hand, might write his or her scripts entirely and then follow them to the letter.

A talk-show presenter may or may not spend time with his or her guests beforehand. It was once the case, back in the late 1960s and 1970s, that talk-show hosts might dine with their guests one or more evenings before the show; occasionally they would refer to 'when we were having dinner the other night'. But times have changed. Talk-show hosts today are not the celebrities they were back then, and few big stars would want to spend their time in this way. And similarly, many talk shows today rely less on the really big names, tending instead to cram a variety of personalities on to the guest list. Dinner with all of these would neither be practical nor necessarily enjoyable for host or guests. A talk-show host today might spend considerably more time rehearsing the comedy links between guests, leaving the conversations with guests to chance, with the help of idiot boards, teleprompters and a pile of notes compiled by a researcher. The talk show as fronted by a presenter who is more famous than most of his or her guests is a dying genre in the 1990s. Instead, talk shows mix comedy, music and chat, and often rely on the host's comic abilities to cover up either the fact that the guests are not that interesting any more, or that the host should never have been interviewing celebrities in the first place.

A less high-profile yet important television presenting job is that of the continuity announcer. The continuity announcer's job used to be simply to tell viewers what was coming up – next, and for the rest of the day; to provide a smooth link between one programme and the next. With the advent of Channel 4 – a publisher-broadcaster rather than a producer-broadcaster (in other words, it commissions rather than makes most of its programmes and therefore has few studio facilities), the role of the announcer changed somewhat. The BBC had already started to use announcers more in voice-over and less on camera (unlike ITV, which still uses some on-screen announcers), and Channel 4, with few studio facilities, did the same. It also started the fashion for using inventive graphics between programmes – which BBC2 has since adopted, perhaps beating Channel 4 at its own game – and so the job of the announcer has largely been relegated to that of providing a faceless voice.

The situation is different at ITV, where continuity announcers have always had a more prominent role because of the regional nature of the network. On the regional ITV stations the announcer will serve to give an identity to the station, mainly linking programmes but occasionally providing other services including giving out local information.

On-screen continuity announcers also play a role during children's television periods, often making a small programme of their slot, reading out viewer's letters, showing pictures and models the children have sent in, and even running the occasional competition.

The announcer's job looks and/or sounds easier than it is. Announcers are selling programmes, so what they say and the way they say it are an important factor in the success of the programme which is to follow. Make it sound dull and people might switch off. Also, like presenters of weather reports, announcers are effectively time-fillers. In other words, they have whatever time there might be between programmes to say what they have to say. So they may have planned 40 seconds' worth only to find at the last minute that they only have ten seconds. This creates the need to edit themselves on the spot. And if the reverse happens – the announcer thought there were only 10 seconds to say what needs to be said and suddenly there are 40 seconds spare – then an ad-lib might be required. This is not easy; the announcer who does it well will be a success, while the announcer who doesn't won't be.

GETTING THE JOBS

Presenters, as we have already established, will end up in television for a number of reasons. They may be experts in a particular field – science or a craft; or they might be famous for something else – being a singer, a writer, a comedian or even an actor (see below). But the fact is, as we will establish later when talking about television actors, that it is actually television which chooses its presenters rather than the presenters who choose television.

You can go some way in helping yourself. You could qualify as a journalist, specialise in a subject and spend your spare time making tapes of yourself presenting some mock television programme. You could sign up for a (usually expensive) presenters' training course which would leave you at the end with a showreel demonstrating your talents. This you could then tout around to television companies, producers and agents explaining exactly what you want to do in the future. It might help.

It may help to train as an actor, try and establish yourself as a stand-up comic (offer to audition at your local stand-up cabaret club) or go into radio (see chapters 4 and 5). Radio can serve as useful background for the job of announcer; many people move from radio to television voice-over work; some do both, their famous radio voice proving an attractive proposition to advertising production companies and television companies looking for well-known faceless voices.

Television presenters Jonathan Ross and Esther Rantzen started life as television researchers (see chapter 15), although if when applying for a researcher's job you seem clearly too keen to get in front of the camera, you're unlikely to be employed. It's good to be keen and adaptable in television, but likewise, nobody wants to take on somebody who plans to spend his or her whole time looking out for another job.

AND HERE IS THE WEATHER

A word about the weather presenters. Most of them are trained meteorologists, who are seconded to television for some of the year and radio for some of the year, and are back doing hard graft at the Royal Meteorological Office for the remainder.

Those who aren't trained experts – the typical bubbly woman or the hunky, well-dressed man – are chosen for their looks or personality and can fall into the job in a number of ways. Oddly, the job of weather person can bring fame, whether the person in question wanted it or not. Ian McCaskill is a classic example of this; his teddy-bear-like appearance and soft, giggly voice have made him a perfect subject for comic impersonators (notably

Rory Bremner on Channel 4), and celebrity has therefore fallen upon him. This celebrity status can earn him places on game-shows, chat shows and advertisements; it can also win him personal appearances (sometimes known as PAs), to open super-markets and the like, and such appearances can be very lucrative.

So even this odd presenting job comes to people in strange ways: you may be a trained meteorologist; you may be a well-turned-out secretary in a television company. Either background can lead to your becoming a television weather presenter, and celebrity status can follow. Or you may sink without trace.

The world of the television presenter is not a predictable or secure one.

THE ACTOR AND THE COMEDIAN

Few actors are ever just television actors. And few actors are permanently employed. Few actors become famous and few actors get rich. That's the bad news. The good news is that whenever they are working, almost all actors love their work, and usually get on well with their fellow workers. Acting is very up-and-down, both where employment and emotions are con-cerned. When it's down, the actor can become very down; and when it's up, the actor will be very up, and it's these 'up moments' (or memories of these up moments) which keep most people in the profession.

The problem is getting into the profession. Most actors have to be trained; few will walk into work if they haven't shown that they have first been able to get into drama school and second, have qualified.

So there's your first hurdle: getting into drama school. It's not easy. You have to audition against stiff competition, and grants are few and far between. Once in, however, you stand a good chance of getting some work at the end of it. Agents are always hanging around the respected drama schools like the Royal Academy of Dramatic Arts (RADA) and the Central School of Speech and Drama (see appendix A), and a qualification from either of these or another school will at least earn you some attention when you go for your first jobs, even if it does't lead automatically to employment. Other colleges and universities not purely dedicated to the performing arts – such as LIPA (see appendix A) – run drama courses, and these would be a good bet if you wanted a broader further education whilst studying drama.

After gaining your qualification, you need to find your first job; and here you'll meet your second hurdle: Equity, the actors' union. You can't be employed as a professional actor without an Equity card; and you can't get an Equity card without first being employed as a professional actor. So how is it done? Well, there are certain forms of employment which you can take on without an Equity card: pantomime; work in certain repertory companies; work with youth theatre companies; fringe companies; and some community theatre groups. If you're lucky enough to be spotted in drama school productions by an agent who feels he or she might want eventually to 'take you on', that agent might well help you through this difficult period to the point where you have earned your Equity card. You are, after all, worth much more to an agent with an Equity card than without.

Once you have a card and an agent (and that is a particularly strong position in which to be), it's then down to you and the agent to start developing your career. You will have to put up with long periods of unemployment, poorly paid work and some less-than-satisfying work (back end of a pantomime horse? Well it's work, isn't it?), while your agent is taking your qualifications, your photograph and your track record around to prospective employers.

How and when an actor gets television work is as hard to predict as any other aspect of an actor's career. Jobs are advertised occasionally – in *The Stage and Television Today* newspaper and some other publications (see appendix B) – but through an agent 'in the know', who keeps up with all the latest news about new productions, who's directing and who's producing and so on, will be as good a way as any to find television work.

And once you get it, it might be the first in a long run of jobs on television, or it might be your first and your last. Some actors get into television and simply stay there; others enjoy a prestigious mix of high-profile television work and the occasional challenging theatre role in the West End; and others get one series or even just a one-off drama and then never see a television camera again.

The nearest thing to permanent television work for an actor is in soap opera. But many don't like the idea of being cast for life in one role. Actors who make a name for themselves in soap

148

opera and then leave to pursue more varied careers don't always enjoy equivalent success elsewhere – not in the UK, at least. There are exceptions: Nick Berry left *Eastenders* and later scored a massive hit in the period police series *Heartbeat*; Geoffrey Hughes left *Coronation Street* after making a name for himself as the loveable lodger Eddie Yates, and has since enjoyed varied work in drama specials and comedy series; but others have left soaps and disappeared without trace – notably Christopher Quentin, *Coronation Street*'s unlikely heartthrob, who failed to cause hearts to throb after leaving the confines of the *Street*.

Abroad the system is different: Australian soap stars have a habit of leaving and becoming international pop stars; while in the US, it is not uncommon for a film star to enjoy a second career later in life in a soap or a sitcom. Such second winds have been enjoyed by macho man Burt Reynolds and even, for a while, Elizabeth Taylor.

Back in the UK, however, actors who become permanent television stars prove to be rare animals. They must perhaps be strong in a particular style of acting which just happens to suit a number of different roles: the late comedy actor Patrick Cargill enjoyed such success in the 1960s and 1970s, as did Richard Briers at around the same time – before he got his second wind as a theatre and film actor. Or, they must be powerful and/or appealing characters in their own right, with the skill to transfer this charisma (or whatever quality it is) to a number of varied but prominent roles: John Thaw (*Inspector Morse*, *Kavanagh QC*) and David Jason (*Only Fools and Horses*, *A Touch of Frost*, *The Darling Buds of May*) are such actors. The actor who is permanently employed on television must be very, very good – an actor for all seasons – or very, very lucky.

Or very, very funny. Comedy is another way on to the television screen, and the stand-up comedy boom of the 1980s and 1990s in the UK has created a number of new television faces. The modern stand-up performers, as exemplified by those who made their names at the Comic Strip, the Comedy Store and other clubs in London – Dawn French, Jennifer Saunders, Ben Elton, Adrian Edmundson, Rik Mayall, Rowland Rivron and others – have excelled on British television as revue artists, actors, writers, performers, producers and in some cases in films as performers. Many stand-up artists who have largely stuck to the live stage rather than turned their talents to television – such as Billy

Connolly and, of the new generation, Eddie Izzard – have often found themselves turning up on television in a whole range of productions, simply because television wants them so badly.

The message, then, for actors and those on the fringe of the acting profession is that talent is a crucial ingredient, and so is luck, but that as a general rule television chooses its personalities rather than the other way around.

21

FREELANCING

Television and radio today are both freelance industries. The majority of people who work in these industries now are freelance, and for a number of reasons.

First there was the recession of the 1980s, which caused a number of companies to shed employees to save money. Then there was the Broadcasting Bill of 1990, which introduced both the rule which said that all terrestrial broadcasters must commission 25 per cent of their programming from independents and the franchise auction which sold off the ITV companies to the highest bidders. The former ruling fostered the development of the independent sector, which employs almost exclusively freelance people, while the auctions forced companies to slim down and save money so that they could afford, effectively, to buy themselves. This slimming-down meant redundancies, many of the victims of which rose up again as freelancers (often in their old jobs), and it also meant a halt on commissions. One UK animation production company, Cosgrove Hall, which relied almost exclusively on Thames Television for its work, had to reduce its workforce from around 160 to 20 during this period. Those 140-odd people had to find work somewhere, and freelancing was the best option for many of them.

So, if you're considering entering the broadcasting business, the chances are you'll end up running your own business too. Because not only do freelancers have to do the job for which they're being paid – director, camera operator, writer, PA or whatever; they also have to control their own affairs, which can be broken down broadly as follows.

Marketing

You have to sell yourself. Once you've completed a few freelance jobs, it can happen that the work starts coming to you, but don't rely on it. A few months out of work for a freelancer can be bad news for two reasons. First, the money stops coming in, and second, once your face is 'off the scene' for a while people start to forget you exist. Out of sight, out of mind. Employers (or 'clients', as you will come to call them) love you when you're there doing just the job they wanted you to do, but they'll have no problem finding someone else should anything go wrong, and little loyalty, either. So it's important to spend some of your time keeping your regular clients sweet, and 'networking' (see below) in an attempt to win new clients. Some freelancers advertise in trade magazines (see appendix B), but this can be expensive. Only do so on taking advice from others who have done the same.

Invoicing

Nobody's going to pay you unless you send them a bill. So first you have to agree on a price for the job – and get this in writing, wherever you can. You then have to put in a bill at the end. This bill is known as an 'invoice', and it will detail not only the agreed fee but also fees for any extra work carried out over and above the original agreed amount of work (these extras must be agreed with the client as you go along), plus any expenses you incurred – such as taxi, train and plane fares and the cost of equipment bought specially for the job and of location meals, etc. If you are registered for VAT (see below), it will also include a charge for this.

Accounts

You have to keep records for tax purposes. These records must detail everything you spend – on which you can reclaim tax; and everything you earn – on which you will pay tax. Your accounts must be clear, and must be verified by invoices and bills, just in case the Inland Revenue decides to check up on you. Some people are clever (or patient) enough to be able to calculate their own tax; most full-time freelancers, however, will pay a small annual fee to an accountant to do all these calculations for them. An accountant can save you money too, simply by understanding the tax system and knowing exactly where and how savings can be made. Take on an accountant and suddenly you're an employer, too!

If you earn over a certain amount annually (call your local VAT office to check what this amount is), you might be eligible to be VAT registered. This is a double-edged sword: you put an extra VAT charge on all your invoices, and the total VAT you are paid by clients you in turn pay back to the VAT office. On the other hand, for everything you buy which is directly related to your work – a camera, a computer, stationery – and on which you pay VAT, you can claim the VAT payments back from the VAT office. Sounds good? Well, yes, and for two reasons: all your expensive office equipment will come VAT-free; and you'll have all that nice VAT money from clients sloshing around earning interest (or providing cash-flow) until your three months are up and you have to pay it back to the VAT office. But what if a client takes six months to pay up? And what if you've used your VAT 'float' as cash-flow and suddenly find it's not all there to pay back? The VAT people (also known as Customs and Excise) are tough. One day late and you can be fined; if they decide to do a random check on you (and they can, and they do) and your records are less than perfect, they can fine you for that too. If you're VAT registered you're an unpaid tax collector who often feels guilty until proven innocent. Another of the joys of free-lancing.

The office

All freelancers, whatever their profession, eventually find they need somewhere to keep their accounts; their correspondence; their invoices; their telephone; their telephone answering machine; their computer (it always helps to have one, whatever your profession); and other tools of the trade. Many start out thinking this can all be kept in the corner of the bedroom. Few successful freelancers end up thinking like that! A quiet work area is essential, be it a small spare room in your house or flat, or office space you rent near to your home, or close to where most of your clients are based. An office needs furniture, and this and other equipment have, of course, to be paid for. They can be claimed against tax – as can the use of your home as an office – but they are still another responsibility!

Time management

This is an aspect of the freelancer's work with which many have great difficulty. Broadly there are two areas where time management is crucial: managing time off, and managing the time allotted for the jobs you're given. There is the danger that if you are freelance you will not allow yourself a holiday – basically because you will not allow yourself the time off. Whenever a freelancer goes away on holiday it is always in the back of his or her mind that somebody might be phoning or faxing back home with an offer of work. Well, this can be planned for. Clients should be informed well in advance that you are taking a break, that you will be able to work up to a particular date and that you will be ready and waiting for work on your return. Two weeks off work can affect your income, particularly if you're one of the many freelancers who work hand-to-mouth, so you'll have to plan for this too – by saving up not just for the holiday but also for your holiday pay.

Time management is also crucial when it comes to juggling jobs in the air. What if two lucrative jobs have come up at the same time? In some freelance professions – writer, for example – you might be able to manage both without one affecting the other. If you're a camera operator or a director, on the other hand, this won't be so easy because you're most likely to be wanted in two places at once. Here is where the freelancer learns a number of key skills if he or she is going to survive! Here you need the ability to play one client off against the other without upsetting either; the ability to weigh up the merits of both jobs – one may pay better whilst the other may be more high-profile and/or lead to better things – and choose the right one; and to learn how to say no to a job (if you end up having to) in a way that makes the client feel that it's their fault you can't do the job! If you are really in demand – and that's how you want to be as a freelancer – one of the clients might delay or bring forward a job so you can do both. That's the ideal solution!

Taking on staff

Most successful freelancers will reach a point where either they stop taking on extra work (and therefore their income levels out and stops climbing) or they take on help. This is a tough decision to make, because few will be earning enough to be able to pay someone a full-time salary, and to take someone on part time is difficult, because the right person will never be available when really needed. Except where secretarial help is concerned. Temporary secretaries can be employed through agencies just once or twice a month if necessary. They don't come cheap, but how much work – and therefore income – can be lost by bad book keeping, and general bad organisation? Secretarial help twice a month or once a week, backed up by a telephone message and paging service (there are many of these operating now – they'll answer your phones, take messages and get them to you without your ever setting foot in your office, for a monthly fee), should be all most freelancers would need to free themselves up for those extra jobs for which they otherwise wouldn't have time.

A sought-after camera operator or highly prized editor, on the other hand, might be in such demand that the money they are receiving allows them to take on a permanent assistant. They would always be able to charge the client for the assistant's fees, so it would only be the overheads involved in employing somebody that the freelancer would have to pay here.

All this, don't forget, comes on top of the actual work the freelancer has to do for his or her clients. What the above list does is help to kill the myth that freelancing is an easy life. It is, of course, very nice ultimately to be your own boss; to be able to decide when you will and when you won't work; to choose your clients; to vary your working week. But all the above 'added extras' do somewhat detract from these freedoms. To be a successful freelancer is a good position in which to be, but many freelancers never chose to be such; they became so because that's how the industry is.

THE CHICKEN OR THE EGG?

Most freelancers get work on the strength of a body of work to which the potential employer – or client – can be referred. But how do you get the first job which will allow you to get the second and third job in order to build up that body of work?

Answer: first get a qualification if you can; then, live, eat and breathe the particular job you eventually want to do – and in particular, get networking.

NETWORKING

Many find this a particularly unpleasant term, and some find it a somewhat unpleasant activity. Because what it actually means is 'hanging around the right people'. A random, non-scientific survey carried out for this book found the following examples of how networking helped a number of freelancers find their next job:

Female, unemployed, would-be TV researcher, aged 23

After a few short-term, usually non-media jobs, I found myself on the dole aged 23. I had graduated a year before, with a good degree in media studies. One of my flatmates and fellow graduates had just got a job presenting a weekend afternoon programme at a local radio station. While he was there one day he got talking to the person in charge of the news and information desk (where all press releases, books and records for review, etc. come in and are redistributed to programme departments), who, in passing, said she was looking for a temporary assistant. My friend recommended me, and I was at the station the very next day, working like crazy to try and prove myself and so as not to let my friend down. When that job dried up I got another in another department, writing short links for the radio presenters. That gave me enough experience to get me a television researcher's job which I applied for whilst still freelancing at the radio station.

Male would-be TV presenter, aged 30

I had tried a number of times to get presenting work, although I don't think I ever tried hard enough. I had done a journalism and radio writing course at college, but was rather unsure then that writing was what I wanted to do. I got to the second stage of an audition for 'new' presenters for a rock music show on TV once, when I was younger, but soon realised that these auditions were a total sham. The main thing they were asking the 200-plus young people who queued down the street hoping for stardom was 'What items would you most like to see in the programme?' Of course, that was all they were after; two of my ideas appeared in the first programme, but I never got asked back for a third 'audition'. (The people who eventually got the jobs were already famous, by the way.)

So I decided to take a different tack and started writing articles on rock, pop, the movies – the things that interested me – for various magazines, and hoped to get noticed that way. It sort of worked; I got asked to appear on radio a few times as a 'pundit', a so-called expert on the music business, but TV eluded me. I failed a couple of interviews for TV research jobs because I could tell they knew I really wanted to present. And then one day a bloke I knew who I used to see with friends occasionally – a TV director – asked me if I'd come and do a screen test. I was to be a pundit once again, something to do with the movies, but they wanted to test me on screen first because the job might involve some interviewing – and even talking direct to camera. I got the job; it didn't make my career as a presenter (I got on telly, but they cut a lot of what I did out – not because it was no good, they insisted!), but the producer told me to keep them in mind for any programme ideas I might come up with and said that they liked my on-screen style. Meanwhile, the magazine articles still pay the bills.

Male would-be radio producer, aged 29

I was unsure whether I wanted to go into radio or print – as a producer or as an editor, respectively. A sequence of events had me wind up as an editor of a magazine set up by a small publisher I knew through friends. His editor resigned suddenly, I'd told him just days before that happened that I was thinking of going freelance (I had just finished a media and education degree and had got a job as a film and theatre reviewer on a local newspaper), and he asked me if I'd take over the editor's job on a freelance basis! I said yes, told a white lie or two about how I worked closely with editors on the local paper, and agreed to start in two weeks' time. Meanwhile I bought books on magazine editing and production, grilled as many people as I could on the subject, and then just dived in at the deep end. Here my colleagues helped enormously. The designer and layout guy knew I was new to this game and steered me through, and we got the first issue out on time, and looking and reading well.

Meanwhile, I had also put the word out at a local radio station where I had once done some temporary research work that I was going freelance. A matter of days after getting the editor's job, I got a call from one of the presenters asking if I'd like to be his producer on a part-time basis, as his regular producer was going part-time. I understood radio – but had never produced before. So I did the same thing and mugged up on the subject. I also went in and 'shadowed' the regular producer just to see what she did before I started. It was a live show, so the first one was a bit scary. But it worked, and what small problems I did have, I got help with from the regular staff. That's my advice: get people on your side and you'll do OK.

These above cases tend to give the impression that anyone can do anything with a bit of luck in one hand and a 'how-to' book in the other. That is, of course, not always so; all of these people had been through college courses – most of them degree courses – so had proved themselves to an extent just by virtue of their qualification.

Another common thread between them all is their willingness just to get in there and do the job. This attitude will show, and will generally be approved of by the potential employer or client.

All the above people were also 'living and breathing the media'. They proved that they were interested, that they had coped in media jobs. They were also moving – or networking – in the right circles. They must also have proved fairly personable and presentable, too. You may feel this shouldn't matter, but it does. The media world is a very social and sociable world; people work closely together for long hours. Prove yourself a good person to be around, and you're half-way there.

SKILLSET

All the above might make the freelance life sound terribly precarious, unstructured and vague – and make the broadcasting industry sound as though it is staffed largely by a bunch of untrained but rather lucky people who happened to be in the right place at the right time. This may be no sound basis for a lifelong career, you may feel.

Skillset (see appendix A) – the industry training body for broadcasting, film and video – is not a training provider but a body whose objective is to develop high standards which define the job roles in the industry. Skillset is acknowledged formally by the government as an Industry Training Organisation and NVQ/SVQ Lead Body (see appendix A), and among its aims are to encourage cross-industry training for freelancers and to ensure courses are made available to them through subsidies.

BECTU, the Broadcasting, Entertainment, Cinematograph and Theatre Union (see appendix B), contributes to Skillset and is assisting the organisation in identifying freelance training needs and putting in place training courses. BECTU also runs an employment service for freelancers in television, film and the theatre. This service costs £5 to register and £1 per week for as long as you subscribe.

So with a move towards recognised qualifications among the ever-growing body of freelance workers in this industry, life as a freelancer might not seem so precarious in the years to come.

BECTU

BECTU offers a number of services for freelance members, including collective bargaining on hours and rates of pay, a telephone enquiry service, representation of freelance views on a number of official bodies and a student link-up scheme which helps students to join the union when they finish college and start work. BECTU also publishes regional freelance directories to help freelancers get work in their region, a producers' and directors' directory and a producers' and directors' newsletter. It also offers assistance to freelancers in key areas, including: copyright, contracts, disputes over quality of work and money owed for work done.

22

AND HERE IS THE NEWS

Where do they get it all from? How is it that, generally, the lead news stories on the ITV news are the same ones as those on the BBC news? Do they copy each other? Are there rules as to what should come first and what should come last in a news bulletin? When they show film of incidents which have happened a matter of hours ago in America or Africa, how and from whom did they get the film? How did it get back here so quickly? When a reporter or newsreader tells us about a crime, a disaster, a miracle – how do we know they have got the facts right?

THE NEWS: WHERE IT COMES FROM

News is gathered from a number of different sources. Most news organisations – like the BBC, which runs its own news depart-ment, ITN, which provides news services for the ITV networks, and in the US, CNN, which provides a nationwide 24-hour cable news service which also reaches many other countries in the world – will subscribe to a number of news 'agencies' or 'wire services'. You will recognise their names: Reuters, PA (or Press Association) and Associated Press are three well-known news agencies. They gather news from all over the world through a network of 'bureaux'. These bureaux are staffed by trained and highly-experienced journalists whose job it is to be on top of every important news story which develops in their particular area.

So, a particular agency's Paris bureau, for example, will have strong relationships with sources inside the president's offices, the French parliament, the various embassies in the city, the Paris stock exchange, and key government ministries. It will also have links with local French news services, comb the French news-papers, and monitor important radio and television services, 24 hours a day.

Similar activities will be going on in bureaux belonging to the same agency, in Hong Kong, New York, Washington, Tokyo, Bombay, Johannesburg, Sydney, Helsinki, London, Amsterdam – any important centre where big news is likely to be generated.

The results of all this non-stop, finger-on-the-pulse research will be a series of news stories which will be put together by the agency's journalists and then sent 'down the wires' to its many subscribers around the world. These stories used to arrive in the many and various newsrooms of the world in the form of telexes which would roll out of huge machines which look rather like rows of typewriters on legs, all day and all night. As the machines clicked away, automatically typing the stories on to huge rolls of paper, 'copy boys' – internal messengers – would tear them off and deliver them to the respective editors of the various depart-ments – city news, local news, international news, sports – who would 'taste' the stories for their newsworthiness and then hand them over to a journalist, either to write them up to 'house style' (all newsrooms have a particular style in which all stories must be written where possible), or to research them further – or 'work them up' into bigger stories, perhaps by adding some interview comment from a relevant figure.

Nowadays, these stories tend to come in on-screen first, and then to be printed out if required. Improved computer and tele-communications technology means the stories don't have to be printed out on to reams of paper; they can instead be sent digi-tally 'down the wires' and straight on to computer screens. Each section editor, and even each journalist, can now have one of these screens on his or her desk – the wires can actually be accessed via a personal computer – so copy boys (they were rarely girls) running around a newsroom with reams of paper to hand out to everyone are now largely a thing of the past.

This is one way in which the news reaches a television news-room – or any other newsroom, for that matter. National newsrooms will also be in touch with their regional counterparts, who might feed stories down for national consumption. News-rooms will also comb the newspapers, local, national and foreign, in case there are stories buried there which can be worked up into something bigger. The 'working up' of a story involves first seeing more potential in something than might be apparent to the inexperienced eye. A local paper might carry a short report about a local man who had to wait three years for a particular operation. A journalist – or reporter – asked to work up the story by a national news editor would try to find that man, and talk to the local health authority, the hospital staff and so on to find out the reason for the delay. The same journalist might then try and find other similar cases elsewhere in the country and then solicit comment from the Minister for Health. This working up of the story has turned a local paper report about an unfortunate man waiting for an operation into a national story involving a government minister.

Such a story is one which can be written, filmed, edited and kept for a 'slow news day'. Unless something happened which made the story time-critical – the man in question died, for example (in which case it would also have to be reworked) – it is one which need not be broadcast immediately. It may be scheduled to feature in a bulletin as soon as it is ready, but it is the type of story which could be shelved as soon as a more important story came along, and still be relevant the following day – unless, of course, a rival television station had done the same thing with the story and run it first. That would 'kill' the story, unless a follow-up report could be put together, expanding on the story or developing it further.

The BBC and ITV have both national and regional television studios, and at the latter, local news bulletins are put together. These bulletins will not be seen nationally, and rarely will they be relevant nationally. On occasion, however, a big story might break in, say, Manchester, where BBC North is based, and in this situation the reports are likely to be put together there and fed to London, from where they will be broadcast nationally. In such a case the national newsreader would read the headlines of the story and then introduce the full report 'from our Manchester studios'.

The big television stations will also have 'correspondents' stationed in key areas around the world. They might have correspondents based permanently in some places – Washington, Hong Kong, Paris, Delhi, for example – and 'post' correspondents to particular places when a big story requires it. These correspondents are always highly experienced journalists and always know their subject inside out. The BBC's Washington correspondent, for example, will be dining out with top politicians most nights of the week. He or she will gather information 'officially' and 'unofficially'. Imagine that during an election campaign a particular candidate looks as if he or she is pulling ahead in the race. The correspondent will know that candidate's best friends and worst enemies; people from both groups will pass on their views and predictions relating to the candidate in question, and these will serve to provide some of the background to the correspondent's report. So, the correspondent will be able to report straight the fact that the candidate in question is pulling ahead, and will then be able to go on to say what friends (named or unnamed) and enemies of the candidate have to say about it. The correspondent will also have researched other campaigns and will be able to give background on what has happened in similar cases in the past. All such information can only come to someone who is there, 24 hours a day, seven days a week, ear constantly to the ground. It's a tough job, leaving little time for a personal life, but it's also highly prestigious and very well paid.

AT THE TELEVISION STATION: THE NEWS TEAM

We've talked a little about how some of the news is gathered and who gathers it; we will now look at the way it gets on the air and who is involved in the process.

The television newsroom generally looks like chaos. Everyone seems to be late for everything; some people will be shouting, screaming, tearing their hair out because it looks as if something just isn't going to happen on time for the broadcast in question; others will be furiously typing away to get a story written on time; others will be on the phone desperately checking facts or seeking quotes. How on earth, when it comes to it, do news broadcasts always look so authoritative and professional?

THE PRODUCER OR NEWS EDITOR

This person is the key to the whole thing. He or she will most likely take control of a number of bulletins on a particular day, deciding what goes in, what comes out, and the order in which the stories appear for each bulletin. The news editor will be under the overall control of the head of the news department, who will be responsible overall for decisions on style, news values and so on and will be called in regularly to discuss emergencies and particularly sensitive issues.

The news editor will have to be very much on top of the news of the day, constantly checking the wires, reading the newspapers, listening to the radio and watching what the opposition are reporting and how they are reporting it. Much of this will also be done for the news editor by an assistant editor, who will report directly to the news editor.

The news editor has the final say over the content of the programme or programmes to which he or she has been assigned. News editors will usually work closely with a chief sub-editor, who will check and vet reports handed in by reporters, journalists and researchers.

REPORTERS/JOURNALISTS/RESEARCHERS

Sometimes all three posts exist in a newsroom; other times all three jobs might be done by one and the same person. The jobs are to research, report and present stories packaged and ready for broadcast.

Some reports will simply be written (from agency reports or from first-hand information phoned-in by correspondents) and presented to the news editor or chief sub-editor and then put straight on to the teleprompt (see below), ready to be read direct to camera by the newsreader.

Other stories might be written in a similar way, with news images added in. These images might be in the form of video footage sent down the wires (agencies provide images as well as written stories), shot by a staff or freelance camera operator or occasionally provided by an amateur. The images might simply be still photographs – often headshots – showing the faces of the people mentioned in the report. Such reports can be written by journalists, reporters or researchers, checked over by the sub-editor and read as normal by the newsreader. The images can then simply be 'fed in' to the report, while the newsreader carries on reading – his or her words becoming a voice-over for the time the images remain on camera.

Then there will be the reports which a journalist or reporter has had to go out and research and film, usually in a limited amount of time. The news editor might have instructed the reporter to get a story on a protest outside a hospital which is due for closure. The reporter will take a camera operator complete with sound equipment, get in a car, on a train or occasionally on a plane and head for the site of the demonstration. Once there, the reporter will interview demonstrators and hospital staff, and maybe a local MP and local residents if there's time, and then might quickly script a report 'to camera'. This would involve the reporter standing in front of the camera, giving background to or summing up the story – or both. Then, satisfied that they have enough, the camera operator and the reporter will return to the studios and edit the piece together, adding voice-over after the edit. This will then be presented to the news editor for approval, some changes might be made (to length or content), and then the reporter will write an introduction to the story to be read by the newsreader. This will be sub-edited and put on to the teleprompt ready for broadcast.

THE PROGRAMME DIRECTOR

With programme content and style determined almost exclusively by the news editor, the director's job on a news bulletin will be to knit together the various elements which go to make the programme – live voice pieces by the newsreader, feeds from regional studios, taped reports from reporters and occasionally remote video feeds for live interviews between newsreader and guests based in other studios or even on location. This will all, of course, be done live, so a tight working relationship between director, PA and vision mixer will be crucial. Occasionally pieces have to be dropped for late news, so the director and PA together will have to be aware how such late decisions, always made by the news editor, affect the timing of the programme as a whole.

TELEPROMPT OPERATOR

This is the person who organises the scripts for use in the automatic teleprompt machine – sometimes known as an Autocue, although the latter is a trade name. This person will usually type out the scripts so that they are properly formatted for the machine – a job done by the PA in most other situations, although in the live newsroom the PA is very much tied up in the control room.

The teleprompt is positioned right next to the camera so that the newsreader can read it whilst looking into the camera at the same time. On occasion news will come in so late that there will be no time to put it on to the teleprompt. In such a case the newsreader will have the story placed in front of him or her, usually in the form of a typed sheet of paper.

THE NEWSREADER

Also known as news presenters or newscasters, these people are usually journalists first, and are elevated to this highly prestigious position after considerable service to television news. This was not always the case, however; it used to divide fairly cleanly down the middle: the BBC would employ people because of their authoritative voice and appearance – sometimes these would be actors – while ITN used almost exclusively newscasters who had a track record in journalism, and they would often write many of their own stories.

This has changed slightly, as the television newsreader's job has grown in prestige. Almost all newsreaders today have some kind of journalistic background, and sometimes take sabbaticals to write books or prepare special reports on faraway places. It's not a job that comes easily to anyone, although there is a new breed of newsreader who will be chosen for his or her relaxed manner – authoritative but casual. Such presenters appear on breakfast and mid-morning slots.

The newsreader has to have perfect diction and clear delivery and must not show any panic under pressure. Newsreaders are faced with sudden changes in running order and script at seconds' notice. The good newsreader will never let the public know this.

GETTING THE JOBS

In this section we will concentrate on the journalists, reporters and news editors, as other studio personnel have been dealt with in previous chapters.

Most television news researchers, journalists and reporters are educated to university level, and not necessarily in journalism. Some will have degrees which include a journalistic component, but there are few degree courses in pure journalism on offer. There are colleges, on the other hand, such as the London College of Printing which offer a range of courses in journalism and related areas (see appendix A).

Traditionally, however, in the UK at least journalism training has been very much workplace-based. The NCTJ (National Council for the Training of Journalists) offers basic journalistic training with hands-on experience, and later specialisation in a chosen area. The courses are still generally aimed at newspaper journalism, but such a qualification would give you newsroom experience which, when coupled with practical experience as a television researcher, would set you up nicely for a television reporter's job.

Many television journalists or reporters start in newspapers or local radio. A local newspaper journalist with a good voice and a flair for radio work is well placed to join a local radio station as a reporter. The BBC runs a Radio Trainee scheme for the training of local radio reporters. Your aim from here would be perhaps to join one of the regional BBC or ITV television operations as a researcher in television news, and go on to national television.

This, of course, makes it all sound very easy, which it is not. A broadcasting organisation is often judged on the quality of its news; none will want to jeopardise their standards by employing less than very good people. You will need to demonstrate sharp journalistic and writing skills plus the ability to work calmly under pressure.

To become a television newsreader is even harder. It is not as if you would be able to get some other type of on-air job in another field of television and slowly graduate to the prestigious job of newsreader; if you had once been the wacky continuity presenter for children's television, this image would never sit happily with that of newsreader.

To become a newsreader you will need to have a background in journalism – possibly radio journalism – and have proved yourself as someone who takes the business of news seriously and who can communicate with clarity and authority. Such people are rare and are therefore paid very well. If this is your goal, you are going to have to work long and hard for it.

The news editor will have worked his or her way up probably from the job of reporter, having showed leadership and editing skills. The news editor will have to demonstrate the ability to be very firm with employees, as meeting exact deadlines and exact standards are crucial in this work. An editor might show natural organising skills quite early on in his or her career; this and a sharp news sense are the most important qualities for this highly responsible and usually well-paid position.

23

TELEVISION: THE INDEPENDENTS

As we have discussed before in this book, the 1990 Broadcasting Bill sent a shock wave of change through the British broadcasting industry. In discussing the independent sector we should remember that it was this bill which did so much to create the growth in the sector of the 1990s.

This makes the bill sound somewhat benign, suggesting almost that it was designed generally to benefit the industry and nurture its equivalent of the 'small businessman', for a while the champion of the Tory government which introduced the bill. But nobody could possibly argue that it was the Tories' love of young, striving producers which guided their drawing up of the bill; the 25 per cent quota of independent productions imposed on both the BBC and ITV was intended as much to reduce the core workforces (and therefore union strength) of both these broadcasting giants as it was to foster the entrepreneurial spirit and to force the BBC out of the pure public sector and into the quasi-mixed economy in which it now finds itself.

Whatever the intentions of the bill, however, it bolstered the independent sector, which had started to grow with the introduction in 1982 of Channel 4, a publisher-broadcaster which, having no production facilities, commissioned or bought nearly all of its programmes from outside suppliers.

So the independent sector as we know it today, which provides many jobs in television, is a comparatively new phenomenon. Having looked at the political background and its reason for being, we will now focus on just what it is, what it does and what it might offer you in terms of employment.

WHAT IS AN INDEPENDENT PRODUCER?

Answer: you are. If you want to be. All you need to do to become an independent producer it to get yourself a desk and a phone and somewhere to put them, and then tell people that you are an independent producer. If you are then lucky enough to get a commission from a broadcaster you simply sit at that desk, pick up the phone and start phoning all the people you will need to make the programme you have been commissioned to make. You'll need a writer to write it (unless you can do that yourself – maybe that's why you got the commission); you'll need a director; a PA; a researcher; camera and sound operators; a presenter; a make-up person; you'll need to hire studio facilities ... but you'll be able to do all that by phone, from your desk.

As this one-person independent production company you will first, of course, have agreed a decent fee with the broadcaster who has commissioned the programme. You will have worked out what the programme will cost you to make – say, £50,000; and you will have asked the broadcaster for say, £70,000. The £20,000 difference includes your fee as producer, money to put into the company to pay running costs (desk and desk light and phone and phone bill will cost, you know), and if all goes well, a little left over to help plan your next production. That's if your production company is going to continue to operate after this particular programme has been made.

It is, of course, a somewhat flippant reply to the question 'What is an independent producer?' The above would not please the many heads of independent production companies who agonise day in, day out over their huge bank loans; whether they've taken on too many staff; whether their office premises are costing too much and whether or not they should have searched for cheaper ones; and, of course, where the next commission is coming from.

But the above description of the one-person, one-desk independent production company does at least explain the basic principle by which the independents operate, in other words, that in theory overheads can be small; that almost all staff can be brought in on a production-by-production basis and be paid for by the commissioning fee; and, most importantly, that an independent only functions once it has been commissioned to make a programme.

INDEPENDENTS: THE INDUSTRY

Statistics published in a report from a 1995 survey of UK independent production companies by Price Waterhouse make for fascinating reading. They show an industry which employs many people but hardly any of them permanently; which spends a great deal of money developing programmes which never get made; and an industry in which many of the companies operating rarely make any real profits. The statistics are such that the somewhat flamboyant, self-styled guru to all entrepreneurs Sir John Harvey-Jones was prompted to ask, during a presentation to the Edinburgh Television Festival, whether the UK's independent producers were 'running a business, or enjoying a lifestyle?'.

Well, let's look at the figures and see. The survey questioned 627 independent producers, all members of the Producers' Alliance for Cinema and Television, or PACT (for which it was carried out), which is the trade association for the sector. Among those 627, 61 per cent were labelled 'small' producers, which means they have an annual average turnover of around £257,000 a year; 20 per cent were labelled 'medium', which means they have an average turnover of around £918,000 a year; and the remaining 19 per cent were the large companies, whose annual turnover could be anywhere between £1.5m. and £16.3m.

So you can see that the majority of independent producers don't make very much money. No problem there; especially if they fit the one-person, one-desk description – and judging by the survey, many of them do. For example, according to the survey the 61 per cent of small producers employ only two 'core staff' members – the term 'core staff' referring to those people who have worked for the producer for the majority of the year surveyed, such as secretaries, administrative staff or other founder members of the company. On top of that the small producers employed on average two people as 'regular staff' – production assistants, researchers, etc. who worked for the company for more than half the year; and 16 shorter-term staff – production team members who were employed for more than two weeks and less than six months. Added together and spread over a year this gives the small production company an average of nine full-time employees a year.

And even when you get to the large companies, there are few permanent jobs going, as according to the survey the average employs a core staff of 10 and 26 regular and 76 short-term workers, which gives a yearly average of 52.

One other interesting revelation from the survey is just how much money the independents lose by developing programme ideas which are never taken up by broadcasters. One way in which independents develop their business and win new clients is by coming up with programme ideas which might interest the commissioning editors. This might be done simply by presenting a treatment (see chapter 16), but in some cases more than this might be required. Researchers might need to be employed in order to be able to present the commissioning editor with sufficient facts and figures to prove that the idea in question is valid; locations might have to be investigated and stills provided to show certain ideas the producer might have for the look of the programme; in special cases a short sample of footage might be required, or even a 'dummy' or complete 'pilot' programme made.

Whichever way or ways the companies choose to develop unsolicited ideas, this process costs the small independent an average of £8,615 a year – that's money spent on an average of 10 development products requiring a total of 66 person days' worth of work. The medium-sized companies spend £14,479 on an average of 16 projects and the large companies, £27,914 on an average of 11 projects.

Interesting points to note here are that the large companies do not appear to develop as many new ideas each year as the others; and that this development money lost by the independents is actually money saved by the broadcasters, because if the independents weren't paying for these experiments, the BBC and ITV companies – and others – would have to.

According to the survey, the independent sector employs just over 12,000 'person equivalents' each year; it produces 10,000 annual hours of broadcasting; it has a total annual turnover of £772m., and PACT has somewhere in the region of 2,500 independent producer members. But given that it seems to be a comparatively low-earning and generally risky sector in which to work, why do so many people get involved? After all, in the reported year of the survey some 14 per cent of companies were making losses, and the average profitability rate was six per cent – which the survey said 'is on the low side of a commercially acceptable rate'.

So many of them must be in it less for the money and more, as Sir John Harvey-Jones put it, for 'the lifestyle'.

BEING AN INDEPENDENT

It can be tremendously challenging, and often fun, running an independent production company. If you are an independent which regularly provides programming for the BBC and ITV networks – or satellite television or one of the major cable companies – you get the best of both worlds. You work for a small intimate company which you also run – and might even own – yourself; you choose your own teams as and when you need them; you see the fruits of your work appear on national television; and, if you're lucky, you make a living from all of this.

For the person running/owning an independent the work divides broadly into three areas: management; research and development; and production. The management is the same as it would be for any company: you have to balance the books, pay for premises, insure those premises, employ staff, pay and insure those staff, sack people, pay tax and VAT, monitor the income and basically keep a well-run, money-making company afloat.

Research and development involves networking with a pool of contacts – directors, producers, writers – to ensure that the ideas keep flowing in. It also involves keeping the commissioning editors sweet. Because unless you've really hit the big time (in other words, unless you're a large independent and have the clout to gather the funds to make programmes without a commission and sell them later, or you have long-term deals with major broadcasters), the commissioning editors are your bread and butter. You will spend long hours in meetings in their offices, or at restaurants, persuading them that your idea is a good one and that they should buy it; you'll spend long hours trying to push up the price they have offered you for one of your ideas; and if you're lucky you'll receive many calls and/or visits from them, asking you what ideas you've got for a series on this or that subject.

Research-and-development time will be spent touting around your company's showreel, looking for new clients and avenues of business; it will also be spent keeping an eye on what other companies are making, what's popular on television at the moment in your particular field and what's likely to be popular in the future.

And production is, of course, your lifeblood. But as you have the other two categories of work to deal with constantly, you might not actually be hands-on producer for many of your company's productions. In which case you might be given the grand title of executive producer for everything the company made – unless the commissioning editor took that title; and then you might be called series producer (if your company made series rather than one-offs), or you might decide to take the producer title and call your hired-in producer an associate producer. With many independent productions, the production company boss/ owner takes the producer's title and employs a producer-director, essentially to direct but also to take on some of the day-to-day production work (which might in turn be passed on to the PA!) so that management and research and development can be dealt with.

WHAT CAN AN INDEPENDENT PRODUCER OFFER YOU?

Answer: jobs! Many freelance directors, researchers and even producers get regular work with independents; some almost feel like – and are certainly treated as – permanent staff (but without benefits like holiday pay, having your tax and National Insurance contributions paid, etc.). If an independent producer is lucky enough to win a commission for a series, and that series is recommissioned and becomes almost a permanent fixture on the channel concerned (BBC2's *Have I Got News for You* is one example), then you as a freelance editor, director, researcher or PA employed on the first series might find you have a job for a few years.

Independent producers can also offer you variety. Win yourself a reputation in a particular field – say, directing outdoor pursuits programmes, or live concerts – and you might find yourself working for a number of independents which make such programmes for various broadcasters.

Independents can also offer you the chance to learn a craft. Many are such intimate organisations that people win an amazing amount of trust in a very short time. If you get an 'in' with an independent, say, as a researcher, but what you really want to do is direct, if you've proved yourself and are trusted and liked the chances are that eventually you'll get your turn. Staying put with an indie can be small-time stuff, but it can also offer you experiences it would take years to enjoy in a big organisation.

A business or a lifestyle? Well, probably a bit of both. And risky, but as 2,500 people (at least) will testify, worth it!

24

FUNDING PROGRAMMES

TV SHOWS: WHO PAYS FOR THEM?

Most people assume that we pay – we the viewing public. They assume that we pay our licence fees and that this money goes towards the making of the programmes – in the case of the BBC at least. With ITV they presume that we pay a little bit over the odds for every item we buy in the shops and every service we pay for so that the people who provide these goods and services can advertise them on television – and the money they pay ITV for these advertisements goes towards the making of the programmes we watch. So we pay for the programmes. Don't we?

Well, it's not quite as simple as that. Not any more. Look at the credits at the end of the next big documentary or drama special you watch on British television, and at some point you will see listed the names of a number of broadcasters or production companies. This list of credits might begin with the phrase: 'A co-production between . . .'. Even the big television event of 1995, the BBC's highly acclaimed television adaptation of Jane Austen's *Pride and Prejudice*, was not a pure, unadulterated BBC production; the credits at the end told you it was produced 'in association with the Arts & Entertainment Network'. The Arts & Entertainment Network, often referred to as A & E, is a US cable channel which presents programmes of a 'cultural' nature. Produced 'in association with' means that A & E put up some of the money for the programme in exchange for broadcast rights.

Any broadcaster will tell you that today it is impossible to fund such a big-budget production entirely from its own resources, and that therefore production costs must be shared by various partners. This can be done in a number of ways.

CO-PRODUCTION

A co-production is somewhat different from a programme 'produced in association with . . .'. Co-productions usually involve producers from more than one country, all of whom contribute a certain amount towards the production costs, in return either for broadcast rights in their particular country, or for distribution rights, or for both. We will come on to distribution later in this chapter.

So, a British independent production company may have in development an idea for a drama series, but it needs production partners to fund it. It has already sold the idea to the ITV Network Centre, but what ITV will pay will not cover production costs. So it takes the idea to a number of potential foreign partners. (Co-productions are invariably between foreign partners because usually a programme or a series is only shown by one broadcaster in any given country. Therefore, it would rarely be worthwhile partnering with another British producer when a British broadcaster is already in place.)

The producer in question may have a number of foreign partners with which it has long-term relationships, and might therefore take the idea to them first. The producer may be able to find the full funding for the programme in this way, its foreign partners able to put the money up by virtue of their relationships with local broadcasters who in turn will take the series in return for a fee – which covers the producer's investment and leaves some profit.

Now, as a co-production, this is not usually simply a financial relationship; the co-production partners, as they're known, will normally want a hand in the production – and this is usually worked out very precisely in the co-production contract. Some partners may simply agree to put up the cash and leave the production to the originating producer. Others will never accept this and will want perhaps to bring in their own story editors, suggest cast members and even change the locations in which the drama takes place. Next time you watch a big-budget drama, look carefully: how 'local'-looking is it? Is it conveniently set in grand, familiar capital cities – Rome, Paris, London – places which viewers in most European countries would recognise? Or is it set against beautiful historical architecture – like the *Inspector Morse* series (Oxford) or *Middlemarch* (the quaint, Georgian town of

177

Stamford in the English Midlands)? Such settings make a drama series timeless, and their historical points of interest or sheer beauty mean they travel abroad better. And therefore they make for perfect co-productions.

With some co-productions, particularly with documentary series, each co-producer might make one or two episodes themselves. Or one producer might take full responsibility for, say, the original English-language version, and another oversee dubbing and/or subtitling – or full reversioning – for foreign audiences.

So, suddenly, in the brave new world of co-productions, we are no longer talking about British programmes for British audiences; French programmes for French audiences; Australian programmes for Australian audiences. Now we're talking about programmes which will suit the international audience – hence the worldwide growth in genres of programmes which travel: documentaries (because local 'hosts' and foreign voice-overs can be used to reversion them for pretty well any country); cartoons (because these are very easily dubbed); and period dramas by well-known authors (because Jane Austen, Shakespeare and Dickens are known worldwide).

DISTRIBUTION

Programmes which may funded from only one or two sources can still earn extra money by being sold on – or licensed – to other countries, or as video products (see below). Broadcasters and large independent producers might well be able to take on this job themselves. The, BBC for example, has its own 'enterprises' department called BBC Worldwide Television, which has responsibility for distribution of the Corporation's programmes on a worldwide basis. In 1995, for example, it licensed more than 14,500 hours of programming to over 80 countries, making the BBC Europe's largest exporter of television programmes. The ITV companies have set up – or are partners in – a number of distribution or enterprises companies to license programmes on their behalf. The biggest of these is BRITE, a sales and distribution company set up by Granada/LWT and Yorkshire Television (see appendix B).

There are also independent distribution companies which will 'take on' any production they feel will sell – or 'has legs', as the jargon has it. These distributors might 'acquire the rights' to a series or programme for a particular part of the world, or 'territory'. So, a UK producer might grant a US distributor the rights to distribute a programme or programmes 'worldwide except for the UK', as the producer would presumably have strong enough relationships in the UK to get it or them distributed there without the help of a foreign distributor. Or, the UK broadcaster who is broadcasting the said producer's programmes might have taken certain distribution rights as part of the deal with the producer; therefore, the US distributor might be granted US and Asian rights only, for example, with the UK broadcaster retaining rights for the UK and the rest of the world except the US and Asia.

It gets very complicated.

PRE-SALES

A producer might also gather production funds by pre-selling a programme or series to a number of foreign broadcasters. Usually a 'home broadcaster' has to be in place before others will follow suit. Once that is the case, the producer (or perhaps a distributor acting on the producer's behalf, or the distribution arm of the production company if it is big enough to have one) will set about the business of pre-selling abroad. Once a particular number of broadcasters have signed on the dotted line and agreed to buy once the production is completed, production can go ahead. Thus it is now the case that broadcasters find themselves buying programmes which haven't yet been made.

FILM AND VIDEO

Both theatrical feature films (films which are made for screening in the cinemas) and television programmes today have a whole new source of revenue from the video market. Ironically this often very lucrative use of material originally made for the cinema or television is often made after the production in question has 'passed its sell-by date'.

So, a film has gone on release and been an average success, but has no life left in it as far as the cinema audience is concerned. Put it on video and get it into the rental and/or retail stores and suddenly it has found an entirely new – and much bigger – audience willing to pay to see it. This audience comprises mainly people who rarely go to the cinema but are interested enough to rent or buy a film (having heard about it through television programmes about the cinema or having read reviews in the newspapers or magazines) once it's out on video. Part of the video audience comprises those who have already seen a film and want to see it again – or if it's on sale (or sell-through, as retail video is referred to in the business), want to own their own copy. It is in the video market that the director's cut (see chapter 19) can help sell a title all over again. 'You've seen the movie as the producers wanted you to see it; now see it as the director intended!'

A comparatively new and lucrative development for the video industry is the releasing of television specials and series on video. Unlike with feature films, one usually only gets one chance to see a television special or series – unless, of course, you video-tape it yourself, which surprisingly few people do except for time-shifting purposes (i.e. so they don't miss a programme which is on when they're out or busy). And broadcasters get criticised for repeating programmes and series too often. Therefore, a number of popular specials and series are now being released on video, and many have sold in such vast numbers that the owners of these programmes have made considerably more money from the video sales than they ever did from the original broadcast. Cases in point are the Wallace and Gromit animation specials by director Nick Park, produced by Aardman Animations of Bristol; and the *Mr Bean* ITV comedy series, starring Rowan Atkinson and produced by independent production company Tiger/Aspect of the UK. Wallace and Gromit and *Mr Bean* videos sell by the million, worldwide. Why these in particular? Well, the Wallace and Gromit films are simply of exceptional quality – but are also animated and therefore easy to dub; and the Mr Bean comedies are virtually silent, and therefore will travel pretty well anywhere. Another reason for bearing in mind the international audience when planning a production.

FUNDING PROGRAMMES: THE JOBS

There was a time when the BBC paid for pretty well all its programmes to be produced, and ITV did the same. There was a time when video didn't exist; and there was a time when most foreign broadcasters were state-run and 'bought-in' few pro-grammes from abroad. There was a time, too, when the BBC and

ITV made pretty well all their own programmes. So, there was therefore a time when people weren't scraping around to raise production finance; when people weren't selling or distributing programmes abroad and when people weren't putting TV shows on video and selling or renting them in shops.

All these new developments therefore mean new jobs. You could be a distributor; you could be a video publisher looking for products to release on video; you could be an agent taking programme ideas around the world looking for pre-sales.

The new jobs which are generated by these new developments are certainly not at the 'sharp end' of the broadcasting or production industries; they are very much more on the sales, marketing and finance side of the business.

Distributors need salespeople to sell their programmes abroad; they also need acquisitions people to acquire productions from producers. You don't have to have any training in production to win such a position with a distribution company; rather you need proven sales and business ability. Therefore, qualifications in sales and marketing now become relevant to the industry.

Producers also need people who are skilled in securing finance and 'brokering' projects – in other words, pulling together the right portfolio of funds in order that a production can be financed and everyone who has put money into it gets out of it what they want. This takes the world of television closer to that of the film industry; all feature films are funded in this way, by bringing investment in from various sources, with each investor hoping for a healthy return on the capital invested. And here also is where film and television differ: investing in television is less of a risk because the return on your investment does not depend upon the whims of a paying audience.

Television sales and distribution might well be one of the less 'creative' activities in the broadcasting industries, but it's probably on the other hand one of the most financially secure and potentially most lucrative.

The sales and distribution side of television can offer quite glamorous jobs. Co-production and distribution involve dealings with companies in many different countries, and while much initial work can be done by phone, fax and e-mail, foreign travel is essential for the development of long-term relationships and for overseeing important co-production deals, for example. Much of this is done by executives, flying from one capital city to the next. Such work is also carried out at the 'markets' and 'fairs' which are held around the world and at which producers and distributors meet, show their wares, strike deals and develop new partnerships and ideas. The principal such markets for the television industry are NATPE in the US (its venue changes annually; it attracts some 16,000 or more professionals every January) and MIPCOM and MIP-TV (each of which attracts around 12,000 professionals from around the world), held at Cannes on the French Riviera in October and April respectively. There are many other smaller markets and 'screenings', examples of which are: the annual BBC Showcase in the UK; the Cartoon Forum, where new animation projects from Europe are screened, bought, sold and developed and which is held in a different European host country each year; and Sunny Side of the Docs, a documentaries market held annually in Marseilles, France.

If this is where you see your future, a marketing or finance qualification coupled with a demonstrated interest in and knowledge of the industry and its products would be useful qualifications. And once you have these, get writing to producers (PACT can provide a list of independent producers in the UK) and distributors, and sell them your skills. Help with where to write is provided in appendix B.

SELLING TELEVISION

Aside from the increasingly complex nature of funding productions, independent broadcasters – ITV, satellite and cable – depend upon advertising for much of their revenue. This involves a team of sales executives whose job it is to convince clients – people with something to sell – that it would be best advertised on their channel. Audience research is an important sales tool for these executives as it can tell clients who is watching what, when, and why and therefore where they might best place their advertisements in the schedules.

A new development in British television broadcasting is the sponsorship of programmes, which can allow one client to identify a whole programme or series with their product. High-profile and very effective examples of this have been ITV's *Inspector Morse* series, sponsored by a brewery (Morse enjoys a good pint!) and the ITV comedy-drama series about a house removal firm, *Moving Story*, which is sponsored by a British bank – one which clearly wants to sell itself to potential home buyers who need mortgages.

Again, sales and marketing experience (and qualifications) will help you into television advertising sales; jobs are occasionally advertised in the trade publications (see appendix B), and writing to the independent television companies (see appendix B) for information about their sales activities would also be a way forward.

25

BROADCASTING: THE FUTURE

When you consider the fact that broadcasting technology has developed at lightning speed since the experiments of Heinrich Hertz, James Clerk Maxwell and Guglielmo Marconi back in the late nineteenth century, the broadcasting industry has typically been slow to adopt these changes.

The UK has had the capacity for five (and actually many more) channels for many years, yet Channel 5 only arrived in 1997. Telstar, the first satellite to send television pictures across the Atlantic from the US to the UK, was launched in 1962, yet satellite broadcasting has been with us only since the late 1980s. And, to leap ahead – and on to the fringes of the broadcasting industry – the Internet was invented in the mid-1960s as primarily an intelligence tool. Yet only now, as we head towards the third millennium, has it become a service made available to – and used by – the mass market.

At last, however, things are speeding up. Whether that is a good thing or not is really not for discussion here. But by the end of this century it is likely, for example, that time-shift television – or video-on-demand – will play a significant role in our television viewing patterns.

VIDEO-ON-DEMAND

Interactivity is a buzzword which you will hear more and more frequently as we move towards the end of the decade. There are many types of interactivity. For example, there's interactive CD-ROM (see below), which involves the viewer, a computer and software on a compact disc; there's broadcast-interactive programming, where the viewer can actually take part in – and influence – a particular broadcast from the comfort of his or her armchair via a two-way communications system with the television (usually involving the telephone and frequently a computer or black box in the home and/or in the studio from which the programme is being broadcast); and there's interactivity, where the viewer can decide what he or she is going to watch and when – a system employing digital compression and a set-top box and commonly known as video-on-demand (VOD).

VOD is made possible by a technological development called digital compression, which, in essence, allows the broadcast capacity of a cable or satellite television channel to be squeezed – or compressed – to make room for many more. With VOD, these channels are used not to broadcast more different types of programme, but rather to broadcast the same programmes at different times. Thus, instead of having only one opportunity to see a particular drama or documentary in any given week, with VOD the viewer gets several opportunities. This dispenses with the viewer's need to engineer his or her time-shifting using a VCR, and so needless to say the VCR manufacturers and video publishing companies are not a little fearful of VOD.

Quite whether the video people need to fear VOD rather than DVD (see below) opens a whole new area of discussion; the VHS videocassette and player is a tired technology, and many replacement technologies have been introduced on to the market yet failed to grab anything like VHS's market share.

The lack of speed with which VOD has been introduced worldwide provides yet another illustration of how the introduction of new technologies doesn't always mean rapid change. The delays have been considerable. At the beginning of the 1990s, key players in the business were predicting that 10 million digital boxes facilitating VOD would be in US homes by the end of 1994. Yet by 1996 there were virtually none. But this is down to the timing of the market itself, rather than the effectiveness of the technology. By the mid-1990s people in the developed world had stopped hurrying for the next television technology on offer. Their VCRs were still recording and playing back, blank VHS cassettes were getting cheaper and cheaper, the video rental shops remained well-stocked, and other outlets – record stores and newsagents, for example – were by this time selling a wide range of videos at reasonable prices. Also by the mid-1990s most people in the developed world were getting over a crippling economic recession, adapting to a new climate in which it was thought better to repay debts rather than wallow in credit, and were starting to think more along the lines of computer technology than television technology. All this and another black box on top of the television for something called VOD? No. In the mid-1990s people were stopping to think about things, and for longer.

PAY-PER-VIEW

Like the National Health Service, television in the UK was traditionally 'free at the point of delivery', until the coming of cable and satellite. Strangely, people will pay not insubstantial sums each month for what are known as 'premium' satellite services (mainly films and sport) and yet will still bemoan the BBC licence fee, simply because it's compulsory. Yet when you have paid your licence fee in the UK, all terrestrial radio and television services are free.

With Pay-per-View (PPV), on the other hand, you only pay if you watch. Such services are now springing up around the world – particularly in the US – but typically are slow to achieve a large penetration. Why? Once again, because people are not used to the idea that the more you watch the more you pay.

PPV is proving itself effective in the case of special 'events' such as the Mike Tyson v. Frank Bruno heavyweight boxing match, for which, in early 1996, BSkyB in the UK felt it could charge viewers over and above the money they pay for the basic service. Such one-offs might simply serve ultimately to annoy rather than satisfy customers; full PPV channels, on the other hand, as long as they serve as complementary services rather than the norm, are likely to take off in the future as long as the programmes they are offering are always something special.

ON-LINE AND OFF-LINE MULTIMEDIA

And then there's the comparatively new phenomenon of the PC, which is considered by some to be a potential competitor to television not only because of the sort of programming it can offer, but also because the PC is fast becoming a real option as a useful domestic appliance.

The personal computer is so called because until microchip technology, the idea of a 'personal computer' was very much in the realm of science fiction. Computers were vast clicking and whirring machines for which special temperature-controlled rooms had to be built. They were used by scientists, defence ministries and multinational companies, and special training was required to program and operate them. Then came the microchip, a tiny device in which vast amounts of data can be stored. These enabled computers to be dramatically reduced in size, to the point at which it became possible to stand one on the average office desk. Today there are 'laptop computers' (the size of a large book) which have double the memory of the computer system which was built into the *Apollo 11* craft, which landed on the moon.

So now we have the PC – which, if fitted with the appropriate disk drive, can play CD-ROMS (interactive compact disks from which the viewer can read text, video image and sound). We can also 'go on-line' with our PCs, in other words, tap into vast banks of video, text and sound information by means of a 'modem' and a telephone line.

To suggest that we're all now playing with our PCs rather than watching television would be misleading, however. In 1996 the world had 1.2 billion television sets as compared with 180 million personal computers, so the PC has a lot of catching up to do. Also, although CD-ROMs have the facility to offer the viewer considerably more in terms of control and choice than your average rented VHS cassette or broadcast television programme, there are still sufficiently few published at the moment for them to pose a real threat to television. For example, in 1996 there were some 70,000 new books released into the stores worldwide, as compared with around 2,000 CD-ROMS.

So if 'off-line' multimedia's threat to television looks some way off, the popularity of some 'on-line' services suggest that they could pose a more real threat. In 1995 it was found that the Internet's 24 million users spent roughly 35 minutes per week, per person on the system, equivalent to the average amount of time a person spends watching video.

Yet what television and video offer the viewer which neither on-line nor off-line multimedia can offer is the engaging and altogether passive experience of watching a programme with a beginning, middle and end – the passive role of the viewer being a crucial element of the experience. But whether television continues to be a mass-market entertainment and information medium because of its passive and social nature (several people often watch television together, which often adds to its appeal) and the PC less so because of its interactive nature and the fact that its use is a more private activity (most people who use a PC do so alone) is hard to predict.

What is also hard to predict is whether or not the efforts of a number of producers around the world – with some help from the techno-wizards – to make television programmes which offer some of the interactivity we're more used to getting from our PCs will pay off.

BROADCAST INTERACTIVE

The introduction of broadcast-interactive programmes, in which the viewer can actually take part in or control a particular broadcast from the comfort of his or her armchair via a two-way communications system with the television, has not been smooth. Because, again, it removes the passivity from television viewing, which is one of its main appeals.

Interactive television programmes are not new, of course. The first to be enjoyed by viewers in the UK was a gameshow called *The Golden Shot*, imported from Denmark and given a new life by comedian Bob Monkhouse who bought the programme format from the Danes in the late 1960s. The programme involved a host (Monkhouse, in the UK), a series of shooting targets and a blindfold crossbow operator. The interactive element was introduced via the contestants, who, watching the programme from the comfort of their own homes, would indicate to the crossbow operator via a telephone where he should point the crossbow in order to achieve the best shot. Once the crossbow's sights were lined up with the respective target, the viewer would shout 'Fire!' down the phone and if the operator achieved a good shot the contestant would move on to another round, or win a prize.

But of course this is not truly interactive television, for in truly interactive television all viewers should be given the opportunity to take a shot at the target. And therein lies the problem with interactive television even today, some thirty years on. There have been many experiments involving link-ups between television studios and telecommunications companies; television producers are creating their own 'black boxes' to facilitate the 'return path' from the viewer's home (usually via phone line) in order that the viewer can interact with the programme in question.

But here we're back to the problems already discussed: how many viewers want another black box; and how many phone lines are available at any one time in order that absolutely everyone who wishes to interact with the programme in question can actually do so?

As we approach the end of the century, telecommunications facilities vary enormously from country to country. Therefore, neither broadcast interactive television programmes (of the type that requires a return path via a telephone line) nor on-line interactive services are going to become truly global phenomena until that situation changes. At the United Nations-sponsored Telecom 95 conference held in Geneva, among the hi-tech displays promising a future bettered by faster and cheaper communications, South African president Nelson Mandela reminded a gathering that half of humanity has no access to a telephone. And at the same event European Commission president Jacques Santer pointed out that there were more telephones in Manhattan than sub-Saharan Africa.

DVD: THE DIGITAL VIDEO DISC

A spin-off from the development of CD-ROM is the digital video disc, officially dubbed DVD in the mid-1990s after the world's key electronics companies adopted a single format in order to allow this long-awaited digital video disc version of the VHS cassette to be developed.

DVD is essentially a CD that can carry a full feature film (or most full feature films, at least – some epics might require two discs). Being a CD, it can carry hi-fidelity sound (of better quality than a VHS tape) and text. The DVD is therefore the natural successor to the VHS cassette – as the audio CD was to the vinyl album.

The trouble is, once again, that it is not enjoying the success which had been anticipated. Who wants to invest in a DVD player while their VHS player is working perfectly well and there are plenty of blank, rental and retail VHS tapes around? And what exactly is on DVD at the moment? And when will the recordable version become a mass-market product like the blank VHS cassette?

WHAT'S ALL THIS GOT TO DO WITH
BROADCASTING ANYWAY?

Answer: all the above new developments represent competition, not only in providing programming, but also for the pound or the dollar in the consumer's pocket.

If more people start spending more time with their PCs, with PPV services or with VOD, the long-serving terrestrial channels such as the BBC and ITV in the UK will start to lose their audiences. To ITV this will mean a reduction in advertising revenue – and therefore a reduction in production and commissioning and therefore loss of jobs. And for the BBC it will simply be harder to justify the licence fee as audiences turn to other programme sources.

And the same will happen to radio. As digital satellite and cable services come on-line offering, for example, presenter-free, CD-quality music for a small fee, so our national and local music radio channels will find it tougher going, cuts will be made and jobs will go. The growth in local radio will also continue to eat into the audiences of the established BBC and independent stations. And meanwhile radio on the Internet – which has become a reality in 1996 – will serve as a new source of work for aspiring radio producers and presenters.

It is not all doom and gloom. The broadcasting industry is expanding. It is true that the growth in the number of television and radio channels is not proportional to the growth in the number of jobs available, but at least this is a growing industry and not one in decline. Also, the spin-offs we have discussed – multimedia, for example – offer those people who enter the broadcasting business somewhere else to go later. People might not refer to this as the broadcasting business for much longer; the audiovisual business might well become a more appropriate term in the future.

26

CONCLUSION: I'D LOVE TO GET INTO BROADCASTING

Like the theatre, the cinema and the music business, broadcasting remains one of those dream careers. Young people who are interested in, say, banking will always say: 'I'm *going* to work in banking.' Young people who are interested in the broadcasting business are more likely to say: 'I'd love to work in broadcasting.' It's as though there is always some doubt that they will succeed; as though so much is left to chance. And it's true that, unlike banking, or bricklaying, or accountancy, or plumbing, broadcasting is a world which you usually enter quite by chance.

But that chance usually only comes to those who are trying in the first place, and that trying usually begins with the acquisition of some sort of qualification.

Speaking as a patron of LIPA – the Liverpool Institute of Performing Arts (see appendix A) – British film producer David Puttnam summed up the plight of the young man or woman who is keen to enter the entertainment business thus:

> No training is a liability; students should have many dreams and as few illusions as possible, quality training enhances the artist without losing the creative spark. However, there is no point in anyone entering the arts without a legitimate burning passion. Why? Because the amount of disappointment, the amount of competition, the number of crises they will meet in their lives, they will not be able to deal with or survive, unless the passion lies there. Therefore, having found the passion, the next thing is to try to hammer in tremendous self-discipline. The nexus of talent is where passion meets self-discipline. If those two things work together, then you've got the chance of being extraordinary.

Much of this book has been taken up with job descriptions, the idea being to give a general idea of what everyone is up to in the broadcasting business at any one moment. The job descriptions are also there to give you an idea of the sort of working life you might experience should you pursue a career in the broadcasting industry and to give you a full picture of what it's like Inside Broadcasting.

But this book, and other books like it, are only the start. It might have given you the confidence to walk into an interview – for a college or university course or even a job – knowing a bit more about what people do in broadcasting. It will have explained terms used in the industry which until now might have confused you. It will have helped you to choose television or radio; documentary or drama; producing or directing.

If having read this book you are still as determined as ever to work in the broadcasting industry, here are some steps you should consider taking.

- Try and make certain that broadcasting is what you really want to do. Be honest with yourself. If you detect any half-heartedness or apathy, then take a little time out and look at a few other careers. Books like this exist for a wide variety of career choices and it's better to be uncertain in private and the comfort of your own armchair than to realise half way through a college course or a job interview that broadcasting really isn't for you.
- If you have decided that broadcasting really is for you, then it's time to go out and buy yourself a large pad of writing paper, books of stamps, pens and envelopes and to move on to the appendices which follow this chapter.
- If a qualification is what you want first – and the experience and discipline of a college or university course plus the qualification at the end of it rarely did anyone any harm – then you must begin to start identifying the right course for you. Using the addresses in the following appendices, write for course prospectuses, make contact with faculty heads, read up on everything that's available to you and talk to as many people as you can to help yourself to make up your mind about what's right for you. Money is always a problem: local authorities, banks, parents and the universities and colleges themselves will together sort out this situation for you, but not without your

help. It's important to look at every option here, from grants to student loans and even the tiring but often satisfying process of 'working your way through college'.

The business of finding the right course, then finding the money to pay for it and then finding accommodation is often more trying than the achievement of the qualification itself. If you get over this initial hurdle, you're in a strong position to go on and achieve exactly what you set out to achieve.

- If you decided to skip college and move straight into a working situation from the start, then you need to turn to appendix B and start writing now to the people you think are most likely to employ you. Without a further qualification, your basic qualifications – GCSEs and A-levels – are going to have to be good. You will also have to prove yourself a well-presented, pleasant and enthusiastic person with lots of drive and a willingness to learn. Here, any 'amateur' work you have done will be a bonus. If working in radio is your goal, maybe you have experience on a school or hospital radio station. You should have evidence of this.

  If a videotape or film editor is a mid- or long-term goal, maybe you have some examples of edits you did 'off-line' (see chapter 19) at home or using school equipment.

  If you're going into the industry 'cold' in this way, you must be prepared for many rejection letters, and you mustn't let them get you down. Everyone has had them. You must also prepare yourself for the fact that your first job may be menial, and badly paid, if paid at all. And you must do every job you are offered in a state of mind which says (a) I'm going to do this job to the very best of my ability, and (b) this job is leading on to bigger and better things. Treat every minute spent in a 'lowly' position as an investment in your future. This way you won't resent the position you're in and you'll do the job with a dignity which will show and serve you well in the future.

- Don't lose sight of your goal, but also don't get tied down by it. Maybe you started off with the single-minded desire to direct television drama. The course your career took, however, led you into a spell of producing. And you excelled – and you liked it. This can happen, and it doesn't mean you failed in your original aims. You can have desires and the passion David Puttnam spoke of, but you can never quite know what you're good at until you try it. If you desperately want to be a director, and nothing else, then that desperation and determination will get you there in the end. But if, whilst on course to become a director, you find you're well appreciated (and making money) as a writer or producer, so be it. As long as you're enjoying what you're doing and always progressing in some way – either financially or in terms of personal achievement – you can never be accused of letting yourself down. And remember that in broadcasting – as in most walks of life – there's never just yourself to consider. Broadcasting is teamwork, and it's in teams where you find your strengths and weaknesses; and it's important to work with them both and not against them.

- Most of all, try and enjoy what you do. People work better and are usually healthier if they're happy in their work. The intensity of so much of the work involved in broadcasting, and the social nature of the work, requires high spirits in all those people involved. Miseries and whingers drag everyone else down with them. Generally if you're unhappy in the workplace either it's time to sort out the personal reasons behind that unhappiness if there are any, or if there aren't, then it's time to move on. And best to move on before your reputation, as a miserable person to have around, beats you to the next job!

So, you're headed for a dream career. If you make it into broadcasting, at whatever level, then you've achieved something that few else in the world do: you've found a job you want and one you know you'll enjoy. And it's a job with considerable responsibility too, because everything you do has an effect on the final product which goes out into thousands – and often millions – of homes, day in, day out.

It's a big responsibility, and it's a privilege.

Good luck!

APPENDIX A

TRAINING AND EDUCATION BODIES AND COURSES

If you have read this book and decided that broadcasting is the career for you, it's time for you to start bothering other people into helping you to the next stage. There are plenty of people around who are willing to do this; you simply need to devote time and effort to finding them. This and the following appendix list people and publications offering advice on training and other aspects of the broadcasting industry.

BBC Centre for Broadcast Skills Training
BBC Wood Norton
Evesham
Worcestershire WR11 4YB

A wide range of courses are open to all, but they are very expensive and used mainly by existing BBC employees retraining or upgrading or those people already in the industry (working with independent producers, for example) whose companies wish them – and pay for them – to undergo training for specific work.

Tel: 01386 420216
Fax: 01386 420145

The British Film Institute (BFI)
21 Stephen Street
London W1P 2LN

The BFI provides the most comprehensive list of media courses available in the UK, through its publication *Media Courses UK*. The book lists courses related to careers in film, television, radio and journalism and costs £9.99. It should be available in most bookshops and can also be obtained via the BFI's mail order number, 01752 202301. The BFI also publishes a pamphlet entitled *A Listing of Short Courses in Film and Television*, priced at £3 and available by mail order.

Tel: 0171 255 1444
Fax: 0171 436 7950

The Central School of Speech and Drama
The Embassy Theatre
64 Eton Avenue
London NW3 3HY

The Central School of Speech and Drama has a strong reputation world-wide, and a success rate comparable with that of RADA.

Tel: 0171 722 8183
Fax: 0171 722 4132

The Liverpool Institute for Performing Arts (LIPA)
Mount Street
Liverpool L1 9HF

LIPA is an institute which has been developed specifically for the entertainment industry. Its central programme is a validated degree which is multidisciplinary and integrated.

Tel: 051 707 0003
Fax: 051 707 2667

London College of Printing
6 Backhill
London EC1R 5EN

Offers courses in film, video, radio, print journalism and other areas of publishing.

Tel: 0171 514 6500
Fax: 0171 514 6577

London International Film School
24 Shelton Street
London WC2 9HP

Offers post-graduate diploma in film production and theory.

Tel: 0171 836 9642
Fax: 0171 497 3718

National Council for the Training of Journalists (NCTJ)
The Latton Bush Centre
Southern Way
Harlow
Essex CM18 7BL

Offers courses in basic journalistic training with hands-on experience and later specialisation.

Tel: 01279 430009
Fax: 01279 438008

National Film and Television School
Beaconsfield Film Studios
Station Road
Beaconsfield
Bucks HP9 1LG

Courses include the National Short Course Training Programme (NSCTP) which is aimed particularly at freelancers wishing to retrain in another area or upgrade their existing skills.

Tel: 01494 671234
Fax: 010494 674042

RADA
62–4 Gower Street
London WC1E 6ED

The Royal Academy of Dramatic Arts, or RADA, as it is better known, is the most prestigious of all the drama schools in the UK, and has a worldwide reputation. The Academy has a high success rate among its qualifying students.

Tel: 0171 636 7076
Fax: 0171 323 3865

TRAINING BODIES

Skillset
124 Horseferry Road
London SW1P 2TX

Skillset is an Industry Training Organisation backed by a number of key bodies including the BBC, Channel 4 and PACT (see appendix B). It is not a training provider; Skillset's objective is rather to work with industry and education in order to establish a system of clearly defined qualifications. As a National Vocational Qualification/Scottish Vocational Qualification (NVQ/SVQ) Lead Body Skillset saw the first NVQ/SVQs accredited in 1994. These represented the first industry-wide professional qualifications ever to be introduced in broadcasting film and video.

Tel: 0171 306 8585
Fax: 0171 306 8372

VOCATIONAL QUALIFICATION AWARDING BODIES

The Business and Technology Education Council (BTEC)
Central House
Upper Woburn Place
London WC1H OHH

Vocational qualification awarding body. Qualifications include Ordinary National Diplomas, Higher National Diplomas and degrees offering particular relevance to the technical side of the industry.

Tel: 0171 413 8400
Fax: 0171 413 8438

Royal Society of Arts Examination Board
Westwood Way
Coventry CV4 8HS

Vocational qualification awarding body. Qualifications include the intermediate and advanced GNVQ in Media: Communication and Production, a qualification for students looking for a broad background leading to further education or employment. GNVQs or General NVQs are designed mainly for 16–19 year old students in full- or part-time education.

Tel: 01203 470033
Fax: 02303 468080

City & Guilds of London Institute
1 Giltspur Street
London EC1A 9DD

Vocational qualification awarding body, with qualifications relevant particularly to the technical side of the broadcasting industry.

Tel: 0171 294 2468
Fax: 0171 294 2400

APPENDIX B

COMPANIES, ORGANISATIONS, INDUSTRY BODIES AND PUBLICATIONS

BROADCASTERS

Radio: national independent

Classic FM
Academic House
24–8 Oval Road
London NW1 7DQ

Tel: 0171 284 3000
Fax: 0171 713 2630

Talk Radio UK
76 Oxford Street
London W1N 0TR

Tel: 0171 636 1089
Fax: 0171 636 1053

Virgin Radio
1 Golden Square
London W1R 4DJ

Tel: 0171 434 1215
Fax: 0171 434 1197

Radio: BBC

BBC Radio
Broadcasting House
2–22 Portland Place
London W1A 1AA

Tel: 0171 580 4468
Fax: 0171 637 0704

(Details and addresses of local BBC Radio stations are available from this address.)

The Radio Authority
Holbrook House
Great Queen Street
London WC2B 5DG

The Radio Authority licenses and regulates all independent radio services, plans frequencies and appoints licensees. It also regulates programming and advertising. The *Radio Authority Pocket Book* will give you details – including addresses, phone and fax numbers – of all independent local and national stations in the UK.

Tel: 0171 430 2724
Fax: 0171 405 7062

Television: terrestrial

BBC Network Television
Television Centre
Wood Lane
London W12 7RJ

Tel: 0181 743 8000

(Details and addresses of regional BBC Television stations are available from this address.)

Anglia Television
Anglia House
Norwich NR1 3JG

Tel: 01603 615151
Fax: 01603 631032

Border Television
Television Centre
Carlisle CA1 3NT

Tel: 01228 25101
Fax: 01228 41384

Carlton UK Television
101 St Martin's Lane
London WC2N 4AZ

Tel: 0171 240 4000
Fax: 0171 240 4171

Central Broadcasting
Central House
Broad Street
Birmingham B1 2JP

Tel: 0121 643 9898
Fax: 0121 643 4897

Channel Television
Television Centre
St Helier
Jersey
Channel Islands JE2 3ZD

Tel: 01534 68999
Fax: 01534 59446

GMTV
The London Television Centre
Upper Ground
London SE1 9TT

Tel: 0171 827 7000
Fax: 0171 827 7001

Grampian Television
Queen's Cross
Aberdeen AB9 2XJ

Tel: 01224 846 846
Fax: 01224 846 800

Granada Television
The Television Centre
Quay Street
Manchester M60 9EA

Tel: 0161 832 7211
Fax: 0161 827 2029

HTV Group
HTV Wales
The Television Centre
Culverhouse Cross
Cardiff CF5 6XJ

Tel: 01222 590 590
Fax: 01222 592 134

London Weekend Television
The London Television Centre
Upper Ground
London SE1 9LT

Tel: 0171 620 1620
Fax: 0171 261 1290

Meridian Broadcasting
Television Centre
Southampton SO14 0PZ

Tel: 01703 222 555
Fax: 01703 335 050

Scottish Television
Cowcaddens
Glasgow G2 3PR

Tel: 0141 300 3000
Fax: 0141 300 3030

Tyne-Tees Television
The Television Centre
City Road
Newcastle upon Tyne NE1 2AL

Tel: 0191 261 0181
Fax: 0191 261 2302

Ulster Television
Havelock House
Ormeau Road
Belfast BT7 1EB

Tel: 01232 328 122
Fax: 01232 246 695

Westcountry Television
Language Science Park
Plymouth PL7 5BG

Tel: 01752 333 333
Fax: 01752 333 444

Yorkshire Television
The Television Centre
Leeds LS3 1JS

Tel: 0113 243 8283
Fax: 0113 244 5107

Independent Television News (ITN)
200 Gray's Inn Road
London WC1X 8XZ

Tel: 0171 833 3000
Fax: 0171 430 4228

Channel 4 Television
124 Horseferry Road
London SW1P 2TX

Tel: 0171 396 4444
Fax: 0171 306 8366

Cable and satellite television stations

Asianet
Elliott House
Victoria Road
London NW10 6NY

Tel: 0181 930 0930

Bravo
United Artists Programming
Twyman House
16 Bonny Street
London NW1 9PG

Tel: 0171 482 4824

Cartoon Network
19–22 Rathbone Place
London W1P 1DF

Tel: 0171 637 6700

CNN International
Turner Broadcasting Systems
19–22 Rathbone Place
London W1P 1DF

Tel: 0171 637 6707

Discovery Channel
United Artists Ltd
Twyman House
16 Bonny Street
London NW1 9PG

Tel: 0171 482 4824

The Disney Channel
The Walt Disney Company
Beaumont House
Kensington Village
Avonmore Road
London W14 8TS

Tel: 0171 605 1313

The Family Channel
84 Buckingham Gate
London SW16 6PD

Tel: 0171 976 7199

The Learning Channel
United Artists Entertainment
Twyman House
16 Bonny Street
London NW1 9PG

Tel: 0171 482 4824

Live TV
Mirror Television Ltd
1 Canada Square
Canary Wharf
London E14 5AP

Tel: 0171 293 2153

MTV Europe
Hawley Crescent
London NW1 8TT

Tel: 0171 284 7777

NBC Super Channel
3 Shortlands
Hammersmith
London W6 8BX

Tel: 0181 600 6100

Namaste
Kingfisher
Unit 3
Trinity Park
Trinity Way

Chingford
Essex E4 8TD

Tel: 0181 523 1442

Nickelodeon UK
15–18 Rathbone Place
London W1P 1DF

Tel: 0171 462 1000

The Parliamentary Channel
United Artists Programming
Twyman House
16 Bonny Street
London NW1 9PG

Tel: 0171 482 4824

QVC The Shopping Channel
Marco Polo House
346 Queenstown Road
London SW8 4NQ

Tel: 0171 705 5600

British Sky Broadcasting
6 Centaurs Business Park
Grant Way
Isleworth
Middlesex TW7 5QD

Tel: 0171 705 3000

Other industry organisations

Advertising Film and Videotape Producers' Association (AFVPA)
26 Noel Street
London W1V 3RD

Tel: 0171 434 2651
Fax: 0171 434 9002

Trade association for producers of television and cinema commercials.

Arts Council of England
14 Great Peter Street
London SW1P 3NQ

Tel: 0171 333 0100

Fax: 0171 973 6590

Government-funded body promoting and supporting the arts.

British Academy of Film and Television Arts (BAFTA)
195 Piccadilly
London W1V 9LG

Tel: 0171 734 0022
Fax: 0171 734 1792

Organisation to encourage high standards in television and film production.

British Film Institute (BFI)
21 Stephen Street
London W1P 2LN

Tel: 0171 255 1444
Fax: 0171 436 7950

The BFI aims to encourage the appreciation and contemporary relevance of films made for television and television broadcasting generally.

British Kinematograph, Sound and Television Society (BKSTS – The Moving Image Society)
M6–M14 Victoria House
Vernon Place
London WC1B 4DJ

Tel: 0171 242 8400
Fax: 0171 405 3560

Promotes development of scientific and technical aspects of film and broadcasting.

Broadcasters' Audience Research Board (BARB)
Glenthorne House
Hammersmith Grove
London W6 0ND

Tel: 0181 741 9110
Fax: 0181 741 1943

Owned jointly by the BBC and the ITV Network Centre, this body provides research on television audiences.

Broadcasting, Entertainment, Cinematograph and Theatre Union (BECTU)
111 Wardour Street
London W1V 4AY

Tel: 0171 437 8506
Fax: 0171 437 8268

Largest trade union in the broadcasting industry.

The Chartered Institute of Journalists
2 Dock Offices
Surrey Quays Road
London SE16 2XU

Tel: 0171 252 1187
Fax: 0171 232 2302

Trade union and professional body promoting high standards across the industry.

Department Of National Heritage
2–4 Cockspur Street
London SW1Y 5DH

Tel: 0171 211 6000
Fax: 0171 211 6270

Government department responsible for arts and leisure.

Equity
British Actors' Equity Association
Guild House
Upper St Martin's Lane
London WC2H 9EG

Tel: 0171 379 6000
Fax: 0171 379 7001

Trade union for performers, directors, designers, stage managers and professional broadcasters.

Gaelic Television Committee (GTC) (Comataidh Telebhisein Gaidhlig)
4 Harbour View
Cromwell Street Quay
Stornoway
Isle of Lewis HS1 2DF

Tel: 01851 705550
Fax: 01851 706432

Independent body, appointed by the ITC, to oversee and promote a wide range of Gaelic programming.

Guild of Local Television (GLT)
16 Fountain Road

Edgbaston
Birmingham B17 8NL

Tel: 0121 429 3706
Fax: 0121 429 3706

Organisation to encourage production of local television, especially through the cable systems.

Independent Television Commission (ITC)
33 Foley Street
London W1P 7LB

Tel: 0171 255 3000
Fax: 0171 306 7800

ITV Network Centre
200 Gray's Inn Road
London WC1X 8HF

Tel: 0171 843 8000
Fax: 0171 843 8158

Owned by the ITV (Channel 3) companies, responsible for commissioning and scheduling programmes broadcast across the network.

London News Network
The London Television Centre
Upper Ground
London SE1 9LT

Tel: 0171 827 7700
Fax: 0171 827 7720

Owned by Carlton and LWT, providing the news service for the London region.

National Union of Journalists (NUJ)
Acorn House
314–20 Gray's Inn Road
London WC1X 8DP

Tel: 0171 278 7916
Fax: 0171 837 8143

Trade union representing journalists from newspapers, magazines and broadcasting.

Producers Alliance for Cinema and Television (PACT)
Gordon House

10 Greencoat Place
London SW1P 1PH

Tel: 0171 233 6000
Fax: 0171 233 8935

Trade association for film and independent television producers.

The Radio Authority
Holbrook House
14 Great Queen Street
London WC2B 5DG

Tel: 0171 430 2724
Fax: 0171 405 7062

Licenses and regulates independent radio services.

The Royal Television Society (RTS)
Holborn Hall
100 Gray's Inn Road
London WC1X 8AL

Tel: 0171 430 1000
Fax: 0171 430 0924

Independent organisation, open to all in the industry, for discussion of all aspects of television.

Satellite and Cable Broadcasters Group
34 Grand Avenue
London N10 3BP

Tel: 0181 444 4891
Fax: 0181 444 6473

Trade association for satellite and cable companies.

Society of Cable Telecommunication Engineers
Fulton House Business Centre
Fulton Road
Middlesex HA9 0TF

Tel: 0181 902 8998
Fax: 0181 903 8719

Aims to raise technical standards within the cable television industry.

Voice of the Listener and Viewer (VLV)
101 King's Drive

Gravesend
Kent DA12 5BQ

Tel: 01474 352835

Consumer organisation representing viewers and listeners on all broadcasting issues.

The Writers' Guild of Great Britain
430 Edgware Road
London W2 1EH

Tel: 0171 723 8074
Fax: 0171 706 2413

The writers' trade union.

Distributors

BBC Worldwide Television
Woodlands
Wood Lane
London W12 OTT

Has responsibility for all the television-related and commercial activities
of the BBC. A major international broadcaster and leading distributor
and co-producer of BBC programmes.

Tel: 0181 576 2339
Fax: 0181 749 8732

BRITE (British Independent Television Enterprises)
The London Television Centre
Upper Ground
London SE1 9LT

Britain's largest distributor of ITV programmes.

Tel: 0171 737 8603
Fax: 0171 261 8162

Trade publications which advertise jobs

Broadcast
Campaign
Screen International
Stage and Television Today
Time Out
UK Press Gazette
Marketing Week

Newspapers which advertise media jobs

Daily Telegraph
Guardian
Independent
London Evening Standard
Observer
Sunday Times

INDEX

Page numbers in *italics* refer to addresses and brief descriptions in the
in the Appendices.

213